GUESS WHO'S JEWISH?

(you'll never guess)

GUESS WHO'S JEWISH?
(you'll never guess)

by Len Chetkin

The Donning Company/Publishers
Norfolk/Virginia Beach

This book is dedicated to
Bobby Chetkin
*a dreamer of dreams unfulfilled.
But more importantly, he left the
plane knowing that he was loved
by everyone who knew him.*

The Donning Company/Publishers
5659 Virginia Beach Boulevard
Norfolk, Virginia 23502

Library of Congress Cataloging-in-Publication Data

Chetkin, Len.
  Guess who's Jewish (you'll never guess).

  1. Jews—Biography—Miscellanea. I. Title.
DS115.C43   1985   920'.0092924   85-13200
ISBN 0-89865-403-3 (pbk.)

Printed in the United States of America

Contents

Preface

In all the years since I was a young boy, I've been excited by the thought of finding out that someone famous was not only famous but also Jewish. It's almost as if I had a rendezvous with destiny to write this book, believing that other people felt the same way.

It was brought to my attention that I would be offending the Jewish people collectively, but being Jewish myself, I knew that was a false premise. My experience has taught me that Jews want to know who is and who isn't Jewish.

The research was fun, because not a day went by that I wasn't astonished to learn that someone I never dreamed was Jewish, surprisingly enough, was.

And even more surprising was learning the unbelievable contribution Jews have made in every field of endeavor. However, in *Guess Who's Jewish*, I've concentrated mostly on the performing arts and sports.

—*Leonard Chetkin*

What is a Jew?

What is a Jew? This question is not at all so odd as it seems. Let us see what kind of peculiar creature the Jew is, which all the rulers and all the nations have together and separately abused and molested, oppressed and persecuted, trampled and butchered, burned and hanged—and in spite of all this is yet alive? What is a Jew, who has never allowed himself to be led astray by all the earthly possessions which his oppressors and persecutors constantly offered him in order that he should change his faith and forsake his own Jewish religion?

The Jew is the sacred being who has brought down from heaven the everlasting fire and has illuminated with it the entire world. He is the religious source, spring and fountain out of which all the rest of the peoples have drawn their beliefs and their religions.

The Jew is the pioneer of liberty. Even in those olden days, when the people were divided into but two distinct classes, slaves and masters—even so long ago had the law of Moses prohibited the practice of keeping a person in bondage for more than six years.

The Jew is the pioneer of civilization. Ignorance was condemned in olden Palestine more even than it is today in civilized Europe. Moreover, in those wild and barbarous days, when neither the life nor the death of anyone counted for anything at all, Rabbi Akiba did not refrain from expressing himself openly against capital punishment, a practice which is recognized today as a highly civilized way of punishment.

The Jew is the emblem of civil and religious toleration. "Love the stranger and the sojourner," Moses commands, "because you have been strangers in the land of Egypt." And this was said in those remote and savage times when the principal ambition of the races and nations consisted in crushing and enslaving one another. As concerns religious toleration, the Jewish faith is not only far from the missionary spirit of converting people of other denominations, but on the contrary the Talmud commands the rabbis to inform and explain to every one who willingly comes to accept the Jewish religion, all the difficulties involved in its acceptance, as to point out to the would-be proselyte that the righteous of all nations have a share in immortality. Of such a lofty and ideal religious toleration not even the moralists of our present day can boast.

The Jew is the emblem of eternity. He whom neither slaughter nor torture of thousands of years could destroy, he whom neither fire nor sword nor inquisition was able to wipe off the face of the earth, he who was the first to produce the oracles of God, he who has been for so long the guardian of prophecy, and who transmitted it to the rest of the world—such a nation cannot be destroyed. The Jew is everlasting as is eternity itself.

---

*Peter Saniford, Canadian educator, director of educational research at the University of Toronto, 1882—. —From an article in the *Jewish Standard*, Toronto, January 15, 1932.

The term "race," as used by him and others, has but a remote connection with its current use in pseudo-scientific theory.

PART I

You Guess the Personality

Test your knowledge
of the Jew in public life

Guess Who's Jewish

*And said, "I made my success
by being mean on the screen."
A top-notch star who* lusted
for life *and won.*

Issure
Danielovitch-Demsky

Kirk Douglas

Born Issure Danielovitch-Demsky on December 9, 1920 in Amsterdam, New York to a Russian businessman named Harry Demsky and his wife, Bryna.

Diana Dill and Anne Buydens were his wives. Each bore him two sons.

He first appeared on Broadway in a play called "Spring Again" in 1941. But it was in films where he made his presence felt.

Brought to the attention of Hal Wallis on a tip from Lauren Bacall (also Jewish) he went on to star in many motion pictures: *Detective Story, Young Man with a Horn, The Bad and the Beautiful, The Fury, Spartacus, Champion, The Juggler, Lust for Life, Lonely Are the Brave, and many more.*

He formed his own production company (Bryna Productions) and produced over 20 films.

On TV he appeared in "Victory at Entebbe" depicting the daring raid by the Israelis on the Entebee Airport in July of 1976. Liz Taylor starred with him.

Guess Who's Jewish

And made her living singing for a cantor. She reached the top of show biz with her TV variety and talk shows...could anyone be finah?

Fanny Rose

Dinah Shore

Was born March 1, 1917 in Winchester, Tennessee.

Arriving in New York just about penniless she made the usual rounds of agents and auditions and finally landed a *non-paying* job at WNEW Radio. However, the *experience* paid off and she hooked up with Leo Reisman's Orchestra and later Xavier Cugat's Orchestra with whom she cut her first record.

Then on to Ben Bernie's Orchestra and shortly after that, in 1940, she was given the regular singing spot on *Eddie Cantor's* weekly radio show.

Later she achieved unlimited fame as star of her own TV variety show and TV talk show.

Guess Who's Jewish

And hails from Alabama yet spent much of his time cheering those damn Yankees. "How about that?"

Melvin Israel

Mel Allen

Born February 14, 1913, Birmingham, Alabama.

Mel, whose career began in 1939, was at one time called the "Voice of the New York Yankees." His "How about that" was as well known as any broadcaster's catchword.

He left the Yankees in 1964 but continued to broadcast football during regular season and bowl contests.

One of the most well-known sports announcers of all time, Mel Allen became a member of the Jewish Sports Hall of Fame.

Guess Who's Jewish

And was tough enough to make James Cagney back up. Short in stature but a tower of strength wherever he appeared. He was the personification of the "Big Town" big man.

Emanuel Goldenberg

Edward G. Robinson

*Born December 12, 1893 in Bucharest, Romania.
Emigrated to the United States in 1902.*

By age 20 he was already on stage and by age 30, in 1923, he did his first film, *The Bright Shawl.*

Typecast as a "mob style" actor as in *Little Caesar* (1930), he finally broke that mold and went on to become one of the most respected of actors of stage, screen and radio.

Some of his more important films were *The Sea Wolf* (1941), *The Scarlet Street* (1945), *The Stranger* (1945), *Double Indemnity* (1944), *Five Star Final* (1931), *Cincinnati Kid* (1961), *Woman in the Window* (1944), and *Key Largo* (1948).

On radio, "Cavalcade of America," "Watchtower," and "Big Tower."

He died in 1973.

Guess Who's Jewish

And said, "I'm afraid of the dark, suspicious of the light and have an intense desire to return to the womb— anybody's!"

Allen Stewart Konigsberg

9

Woody Allen

Born December 1, 1935 in Flatbush, Brooklyn, New York.

Infatuated with comedy, he sent one-liners to Walter Winchell and Earl Wilson who, amazingly, used them. He was only 15 at the time.

By 1952, he was 17, he was a staff writer at NBC and at 21, won a Sylvania Award for a show he wrote for Sid Caesar.

By 1960 he was earning $1,700 a week writing for the Garry Moore Show.

Restless, he began looking for other areas to channel his talent. It was then that he turned to performing. He started in a club in Greenwich Village called the Duplex and by 1964 he was earning five figures per performance in nightclubs all over the U.S. That same year he made the film, *What's New Pussycat?* with Peter Sellers.

He then made *Casino Royale* which got him into the big time.

Woody got the stage bug and *hit* with his play *Don't Drink the Water*. (He was the playwrite.)

And hit again with *Play It Again, Sam* with Diane Keaton (who became his wife and a dominant figure in his life.)

By this time he had married Louise Lasser and divorced her in 1969.

Woody's more important films were *Bananas* (1971), The Film— *Play It Again, Sam* (1972), *Everything You Always Wanted to Know About Sex But Were Afraid to Ask* (1973), *Annie Hall* (1977), *Interiors* (1978), *Manhattan* (1979), and *Zelig* (1983).

Guess Who's Jewish

And said, "Do me a favor, will ya, Harry? Drop dead!" The Bells will always ring for Judith.

Judith Tuvim

Judy Holiday

Born 1923 in New York City.

Judy got her start playing a telephone operator in a play with Orson Welles.

Then she toured with a nightclub act called the Revuers using her real name Judith Tuvim.

The success of the Revuers led to motion pictures when she appeared in *Something for the Boys* and *Winged Victory.*

Her first New York appearance was the Belasco Theatre March 20, 1945 as Alice in "Kiss Them for Me."

In 1946 she was a collosal hit as Billie Dawn in "Born Yesterday," staying with the play through most of its 1,000 performances. On screen she played the same part (with Broderick Crawford) and won an Academy Award.

Then came "Bells are Ringing" and a New York Drama Critics Award.

Judy died in 1965 a victim of cancer.

Guess Who's Jewish

And said, "I like guys who verbalize more than guys who physicalize." She was zaftik (shapely, succulent), to be sure.

Tina Blacker

Tina Louise

Born in 1937, in New York City.

She grew up to be one of the loveliest ladies on film and television.

"It's better to show your brains than your bosom," she once was quoted as saying.

But in spite of that quote, it wasn't her brain that got her a starring role in "Gilligan's Island," her TV super hit.

Prior to TV she appeared in "L'il Abner" on Broadway (capitalizing again on you know what!)

And *God's Little Acre* on film (ditto).

Guess
Who's
Jewish

And started life as a "rosebud." Asked what part of her anatomy got her into films, she replied, "I always used to say my "can," can.

Miss Rosebud
Blustein

Joan Blondell

Born August 13, 1909 in New York City.

Joan Blondell was a wisecracking breezy, gum chewing blonde who got her first lead on film in 1931 in "Blonde Crazy" with James Cagney.

Enormously popular, she set a record making 32 films in 27 months.

Popular as she was, she was not an award winner.

She once said, "My 'can' can got me into the film business."

Some of her films were *The Crowd Roars* (1932), *Dames* (1934), *Stage Struck* (1936), *Stand-In* (1937), *A Tree Grows in Brooklyn* (1945), *Opening Night* (1948), and *Cincinnati Kid* (1965). She appeared in numerous other movies.

Guess Who's Jewish

And married the legendary Mr. Higgins of My Fair Lady. She gave her body and soul to Garfield (on film, that is).

Maria Peiser

Lily Palmer

Born May 24, 1914 in Posen, Germany to Dr. Alfred Peiser and his wife Rose (Lissman).

In 1943, she married Rex Harrison and starred with him in *Belle Book and Candle.*

She also starred in *Caesar and Cleopatra* on stage.

On film she starred in *Notorious Gentleman, Cloak and Dagger, Beware of Pity, Body and Soul* (with John Garfield), *My Girl Tisa,* and many others.

Guess Who's Jewish

And said, "I owe it all to Angelo Petri, the director of a school for problem children." Dead at 40, they say he made "love" one too many times.

Julius Garfinkel

John Garfield

Born May 21, 1912 to David and Hanna Garfinkel.

His first break came as a member of a road company of "Counsellor at Law." He later played the same role on Broadway alongside Paul Muni.

He then signed with Warner Brothers and went on to make many films, such as *Having a Wonder Time, Body and Soul, Postman Always Rings Twice, Humoresque, Four Daughters, Golden Boy,* and *Gentlemen's Agreement.*

John Garfield died in 1952. Rumor has it he was making love at the time.

Guess Who's Jewish

And found that for those who persevere there is always "room at the top." An international star, she was born in Germany.

Simone Kaminker

Simone Signoret

Born in 1921 in Weisbaden, Germany.

Her father was a Polish Jew. Her mother, a French non—Jew.

Provocative, intelligent and caring person who rose to stardom on the wings of a smoldering feminity on screen and a huge dramatic talent. Some of her vehicles include *Casqu d'or*, *Room at the Top*, *Ship of Fools*, *Salt of the Earth*, *Paris Match*, *The Confession*, *The Crucible*, and *Zorba the Greek*.

The love of her life was Ivo Levi, a French Jew.

Guess Who's Jewish

And whose taste runs to Italian men. She married two. Her star burned brightly despite a 75-lb. weight gain.

Shirley Schrift

Shelly Winters

Born August 18, 1922 in St. Louis, Missouri.
Her father was Jonas Schrift and her mother Rose.

Shirley married twice. Once to an Italian American and once to an Italian.

She first appeared on stage in 1930. It was in Jamaica, Long Island in a play titled *Waiting for Lefty* by Cliff Odets.

Since then she has appeared in numerous productions on stage, film and TV.

No one made the transformation from svelte to hefty more successfully than Shelly.

She was married to Vittorio Gassman and later to Anthony Francioso. Both marriages ended in divorce.

On Broadway stage Shelly starred as Ado Annie in *Oklahoma*; Celia Pope in *Hatful of Rain*; Hilda Brookman in *Girls of Summer*; and Maxine Faulk in *Night of the Iguana*.

On film her finest hours were in *A Double Life*, *The Great Gatsby*, *A Place in the Sun*, *I Am a Camera*, *The Poseidon Adventure*, *A Patch of Blue*, and *Diary of Anne Frank*.

Guess Who's Jewish

And French, and made love to Marilyn Monroe (on screen, that is) and Simone Signoret (off screen, that is); or was it the other way around?

Ivo
Levi

Yves Montand

Born in Italy, October 13, 1921.
Yves moved to Marseilles to flee Mussolini.

At 18, he was singing in music halls and was lucky enough to become the protege of Edith Piaf who helped him to land an important role in *Les Portes de la Nuit*, a film made in France. That proved to be Yves' vehicle to stardom.

In 1951, he married Simone Signoret (who called him the love of her life). He didn't return the compliment.

After many films made in France he tried Hollywood with little success. Some say that his on-screen romance with Marilyn Monroe during the filming of *Let's Make Love* exploded into a full-blown off-screen romance. If true, it was a short-lived little fling at best. Soon after, Yves returned to France and resumed his career in films produced by Continental film makers.

But, in 1983 he returned to the United States, New York City in particular, and wowed the Big Apple with a *smash hit one-man performance* at the Metropolitan Opera House.

Now, he's back in France and considered the elder statesman of the French film industry.

Guess Who's Jewish

And became half of one of the greatest comedy teams ever. For many people, the story ended there. It all began in Atlantic City.

Joseph Levitch

27

Jerry Lewis

Born March 6, 1926 to Danny and Mona Levitch, two Vaudeville performers who adopted the name Lewis.

Jerry is a skilled comedian who, in our opinion, has never been given the appreciation he deserves.

He's had his hits and he's had his mis-hits, but the comedic material was always there.

The team of Dean Martin and Jerry Lewis took the country by storm. There was always an anticipation by the audience of what was in store. They were seldom disappointed.

Taking the God's eye view, Jerry Lewis, who started in 1931 singing "Brother Can You Spare a Dime," must be considered one of the brightest stars in the acting comedy field.

Some of his films were *My Friend Irma*, *The Caddy*, *At War with the Army*, *Pardners*, *Cinderfella*, and *Disorderly Orderly*; and his most recent film, *The King of Comedy*, his first straight role, something many people have waited for, proved to be the successful venture anticipated by his fans.

Guess Who's Jewish

And was brought to public attention as the evil daughter of an Egyptian seeress. Actually, she was from Cincinnati, Ohio, and was a top box office smash of silent days.

Theodosia Goodman

Theda Bara

Born in 1890 in Cincinnati, Ohio.

Theda was "The Vamp," the top box office smash of her time who made 39 films in four years.

Her first film was *A Fool There Was.*

Her best films were *Carmen* (1915), *Camille* (1917, her number one film), *Cleopatra* (1917), *Madame Dubarry* (1918), and *Salome* (1918).

Theda was one of the first stars to have an image totally manufactured in Hollywood. The girl from Cincinnati became the evil daughter of an Egyptian seeress. The public bought it. They wanted to buy it. "Glamour" was in. Hollywood gave it to them and everybody ended up happy. Theda Bara died in 1955.

Guess Who's Jewish

And hit stardom cavorting in a film with a frolicsome mini-hobo. She married him.

Pauline Marion Levee

Paulette Goddard

Born in Great Neck, Long Island, June 13, 1911.
She took her mother's maiden name as her stage name (Goddard).

Pauline had an impressive array of husbands: Charlie Chaplin, Burgess Meredith, and Erich Maria Remarque.

Starring with Chaplin after being a Ziegfeld girl and a Hal Roach protege, she really hit the top when she appeared with Bob Hope in *The Cat and the Canary.*

Some of her other films were *The Women* (1939), *Ghost Breakers* (1940), *Hold Back the Dawn* (1941), *Reap the Wild Wind* (1942), and *Kitty* (1945).

I think of her as the absolutely stunning woman who just "missed" in Hollywood.

Guess Who's Jewish

And owes it all to mama, who hardly ever missed a performance. Uncle Yuhkl (buffoon).

Milton Berlinger

Milton Berle

Born July 12, 1908 in Harlem, New York. Father, Moses Berlinger. Mother, Sarah Glantz.

Milton's childhood ended at five years of age when he won a Charlie Chaplin contest.

Then, with mama running interference, he got his first job, a spot in *Perils of Pauline*.

A host of kid parts followed and a shot at working with Mary Pickford, Chaplin and Flora Finch.

Mama kept Milton busy—working wherever she could find him a job. Finally they landed in Hollywood and Milton appeared in *New Faces of 1937*.

Milton made many films. Among them were *A Gentleman at Heart* (1941), *Margin for Era* (1942), *Nose to Nose* (1941), and *Whispering Ghosts* (1942).

Not a very awe-inspiring line-up. It was as Uncle Miltie on the Texaco Star Theatre that fame found Milton Berle. He was "Mr. Television" for seven years and went on to become one of those personalities, highly respected, who weathered the ravishing of the decades. Milton remains at the upper echelons of show business even today.

Guess Who's Jewish

And got some of his biggest laughs by not answering his valet. He "played" the violin.

Benjamin Kubelsky

Jack Benny

Born on February 14, 1894 in Chicago, Illinois (not Waukeegan) to Meyer and Emma Kubelsky (Sachs).

At the age of sixteen, Jack teamed up with Cora Salisbury and formed the team "Salisbury and Benny, from Grand Opera to Ragtime." Jack, of course, was playing violin and spoke nary a word.

After Cora left the act, the gap was filled by Lyman Woods, which was the way the act remained until Jack enlisted in the Navy. It was in a naval theatrical group that Jack spoke his first words on stage.

Jack Benny always said, "It's what you do when you *come on* that carries the act—you can always get off." One of his famous opening lines was, "I'd give a million to know what I look like."

Jack married Sadie Marks January 14, 1927. She later joined the act for a few years (Mary Livingstone).

Truly a giant in show business, he starred on radio, television, theatre, films, and night clubs.

Jack died December 26, 1974.

His passing left a void never to be filled.

Guess Who's Jewish

And was the son of a religious figure. He made millions by getting down on one knee. He introduced the "talkies" to the world.

Asa Yoelson

Al Jolson

Was born May 16, 1886 in St. Petersburg, Russia.
"You ain't heard nothin' yet," was his favorite line. A tireless performer who would perform at parties to the early hours after doing three hours on Broadway.

I call him the "greatest of all times."

Son of a cantor, who wanted him to follow in his footsteps, Jolson ran away from home to try the stage and eventually became a top Vaudeville performer. Working in blackface and kneeling on one knee were two of his favorite gimmicks.

Jolson could make you laugh, and then have you crying within minutes. *Nobody* could sell a song like Jolie and he proved it over and over again.

In *The Jazz Singer*, one of the first "talkie" films, he sang "My Mammy" and had a runaway hit on his hands.

Following up, he appeared in *The Singin' Fool* and tore up the audience with "Sonny Boy."

The Jolson Story (Jolson did the singing to Larry Parks lip synch) was the most popular biographical film ever produced.

Jolson Sings Again was almost as popular.

Al Jolson passed away in 1950.

I've always missed him.

Guess Who's Jewish

And has the most fantastic set of legs to ever grace the screen, to ever hit the stage, to ever traverse a runway, to ever...

Tula Ellice Finklea

Cyd Charisse

Born March 8, 1921 in Amarillo, Texas.
One of the great female dancers on film.

Fred Astaire once said, "She is Beautiful Dynamite."

Her nickname was Cyd and the Charisse came from her first husband.

She later married Tony Martin (Al Morris) and remains with him. He too is Jewish.

Some of her films were *Singin' in the Rain* (Gene Kelly, 1952), *Meet Me in Las Vegas* (Dan Dailey, 1956), *Silk Stockings* (Fred Astaire, 1957), *Brigadoon* (1954), and *The Band Wagon* (1953).

Guess Who's Jewish

And not the greatest golfer in the world... However, she did get herself a bogie. She said, "Just put your lips together and blow."

Betty Jane Perske

Lauren Bacall

Born September 16, 1924 in New York City.

At 19 she made her debut in films in *To Have and Have Not* with Humphrey Bogart—who flipped over her, and being a bright fellow, wooed and wed her.

In 1945 they were together again in *The Big Sleep.*

Her famous line (teaching Bogart how to whistle), "Just put your lips together and blow," still wows the public.

Bogart died in 1957 and Lauren later married Jason Robards in 1961, and divorced him in 1969.

Some of her films were *Dark Passage, How to Marry a Millionaire*, and *Key Largo.*

She starred in many others.

More importantly, don't forget her Broadway hit—*Woman of the Year.*

Guess Who's Jewish

And died in a tragic plane crash en route from Spain to England in 1943. Gone with the wind.

Leslie Stainer

Leslie Howard

Born in London, England on April 3, 1893, Leslie Howard died in a tragic plane crash en route from Spain to England during World War II.

Rumor has it that the Germans thought Winston Churchill was on the plane.

It was in 1916 that Leslie married Ruth Martin and unlike many show biz marriages, he was still married to her at the time of his death (1943).

They were a very close family. His children, Winkie (son) and Doodie (daughter) were an integral part of his life.

Famous on stage and screen, he appeared with the cream of the profession. Names like Hayes, Cornell, Bankhead, Pickford, Davis, Shearer, Bergman, Leigh, and Davis lit up the marquee alongside Leslie's.

Some of his films were *Gone With the Wind, Hamlet, Pygmalion, Intermezzo, The Animal Kingdom, Charley's Aunt,* and *Escape.*

Guess Who's Jewish

And was so desperate that when she got an obscene phone call she said, "Hold on a minute." A natural to replace Johnny Carson.

Joan Molinsky

Joan Rivers

Born in 1935 to Dr. and Mrs. Meyer Molinsky in Brooklyn, New York.

The Johnny Carson Show was her vehicle to stardom. But prior to that she wrote material for Phyllis Diller, Bob Newhart, Phil Foster and Zsa Zsa Gabor.

She has been described as the most intuitively funny woman alive, and her star is still rising at this printing.

If Johnny were to step down, it would seem to me that Joan Rivers could hold that spot better than any person on the talk show scene today.

Guess Who's Jewish

And said, "No matter what the price of corn, this is one ear who never sold himself cheap in the marketplace of filmdom." A rough, tough cookie on film.

L.J.C.

Lee J. Cobb

Born December 9, 1911, died 1976. His father was Benjamin Jacob Cobb. His mother, Kate (Heilecht) Cobb.

Once described as one of the world's great actors, Lee J. Cobb ran the gamut of character portrayals on film as well as on stage. It wasn't easy. Before he could wedge a foot inside the door it took selling radio tubes on commission, studying accounting at CCNY and numerous trips to California until he was finally accepted at the Pasadena Playhouse, where he acted and directed for three years.

It was on stage in New York playing Father Bonaparte in *Golden Boy* that proved to be Lee's big breakthrough. With that part under his belt, things started falling in place. As a member of the Theatre Guild he appeared in numerous productions and alternated between screen and legit for a few years.

In 1949 Arthur Miller's play *Death of a Salesman* was brought to Broadway. Lee won the part of Willie Loman, the ill-fated traveling salesman and with it wrote a piece of Broadway history never to be forgotten.

Turning back to the movies, he starred in a host of nondescript films until he accepted the role of the union mobster Johnny Lately in *On The Waterfront*. I've always considered it his greatest triumph.

Guess Who's Jewish

And said, "I'll bet you think I made it in Hollywood because of a gorgeous face and fantastic body. Maybe you're right. But, I've been chuckin' around this business since I'm six years old." A stunning entertainer who never quite hit the top.

Jill Oppenheim

Jill St. John

Born August 19, 1940 in Los Angeles, California.
Jill got her education at UCLA. Too bad they didn't get a chance to teach her that marriage at an early age rarely works. She had married number one by the time she entered school (Neil Durbin). Duration, two years. After a year of singleness, Jill took another shot (Lance Reventlow). Duration, three years. Jack Jones soon became number three, but only for two years.

Still, in her defense I must say when you're that young and that stunning a woman, marriage seems to find its way into your life. Jill's was no exception.

By the time she was 16, Jill St. John had appeared on over 1,000 radio shows and over 50 TV programs.

In 1959 she made her first movie, *Summer Love*. Many followed. Mostly of the so-so variety. Her experience eventually will bring the artistic success all entertainers are seeking. I wish her good luck.

Some other films she appeared in were *Holiday for Lovers* (1959), *The Lost World (1960)*, *Roman Spring of Mrs. Stone* (1961), *Come Blow Your Horn* (1962), *The Liquidator* (1965), and *Tony Rome* (1967).

Guess Who's Jewish

And used his psychic ability to eliminate negative images of himself and went on to win the highest award in his field. The oddity is he used his curves to as great advantage as so many glamorous film stars have done.

S.S.

Steve Stone

Born July 14, 1947 in Cleveland, Ohio.
Steve was an all-around athlete who settled on baseball for his career. After three years in the minors, it was the Giant organization who brought him to the majors. By the time he hung up his spikes he had played for White Sox, Cubs and Orioles. While with the Orioles, Steve won the Cy Young Award with a 25-7 record. His lifetime wins and losses were 107-93 with a 3.96 ERA.

Steve now broadcasts for my beloved Chicago Cubs.

Guess Who's Jewish

Her big break in show biz came when she lost her make-up kit and had to perform without blackface. Last of the red-hot mamas.

Sophie Abruzza

Sophie Tucker

Sophie was born in 1884 in a wagon leaving Russia. She was on her way to America to join her father, who had changed his name to Abruzza to gain entry into America. Sophie was three months old when she came to Boston.

At 16, she eloped with a man named Louis Tuck with whom she had a son, Bert.

Six years later she turned up in New York City with a new name, Tucker, and a new ambition, 'show biz.'

Performing in blackface she started in a small club in NYC and soon was playing towns all over Pennsylvania, New York and New Jersey.

It was on the Borsht Beat in one of the little towns that all entertainers hit at one time or another during their careers, that Sophie got lucky. She got lucky by losing something. *Her make-up kit.* And was forced to perform without blackface. The audience loved her and the blackface was laid to rest forever.

Sophie went on to become one of the brightest stars of stage and screen.

"Some of These Days" became her theme song and stuck with her throughout her career.

Sophie Tucker died in 1966.

She was truly the last of the Red-Hot Mamas.

Guess Who's Jewish

And said, "Didn't anybody notice me in Bonnie and Clyde?" *If you talk about Mel Brooks and Woody Allen, how can you omit him?*

Jerome Silberman

Gene Wilder

Born June 11, 1935 in Milwaukee, Wisconsin of a Russian Jewish father and a Chicago-born mother.

Gene's initial attempt at acting was in a production of *Romeo and Juliet* at the Milwaukee Playhouse in 1948.

Dissatisfied with his training as an actor, he opted for the old Vic Theatre in Bristol, England then returned to the U.S. only to be inducted into the Army where he served at Valley Forge Army Hospital.

After his discharge, he resumed his surge to movie stardom and achieved wide success as a writer, producer and actor. Some of his funniest moments on film were in *Young Frankenstein, Blazing Saddles, The World's Greatest Lover*, and *The Adventures of Sherlock Holmes' Smarter Brother*.

Guess Who's Jewish

And said, "I rode freight trains for kicks, got beat up for laughs, cut grass for quarters and sang for dimes." He's been likened to Tom Paine and Huck Finn.

Robert Zimmerman

Bob Dylan

Born May 24, 1941 in Duluth, Minnesota.

In folk music, Dylan has no peer—he stands alone. He stands against racial intolerance, he stands against war, and he stands against poverty. His songs tell you that. "Blowin' in the Wind" tells you that.

As a boy he was consumed with the desire to tell the world how he felt about it. So he mastered the guitar, then left home in 1960 heading for New York where he sang his messages to the masses. He played Greenwich Village coffee houses for nickles and dimes. By now he had changed his name to Dylan due to the tremendous influence on him by Dylan Thomas.

Religion doesn't justify war and a few more jobs don't justify munition making.

He writes what he feels about life, about injustice, about inhumanity, about people, and how they feel...and what they need...and who they are.

He's a giant who doesn't throw his weight around. Unless it's to open up eyes and hearts.

Guess Who's Jewish

And said to Bogart, "You despise me don't you?" and Bogie replied, "Well, if I gave you any thought, I probably would." Mr. Moto.

Laszlo Loewenstein

Peter Lorre

Born June 26, 1904. Died in 1974.
Peter played the despicable character so charmingly that audiences ended up loving him. No matter how they tried to make him the villain, hated and despised by all, it just wouldn't fly. In the end Peter's charm never petered out.

He stole scenes regularly from the featured stars in films he appeared in. And movie fans showed up in droves often not realizing it was Lorre they were there to see.

M was his first film (1931). *The Patsy* was his last (1964). In between he appeared in dozens more.

His more well-known films were *The Maltese Falcon, Casablanca,* and *Mr. Moto.*

Guess Who's Jewish

And entertained children all over the world. He sings. He dances. And once led a secret life.

David Kominski

Danny Kaye

Born July 18, 1913 in Brooklyn, New York. His father, Jacob, was a tailor who had emigrated from Russia.

Like virtually all Jewish comedians, Danny played the Borscht Circuit. But unlike most Jewish comedians, he reached the top echelons of Show Biz. A star of stars. Broadway, on film, radio and television, no corner of the business escaped him. Yet Danny Kaye is most remembered for his worldwide work with children. His untiring effort to bring the plight of under-privileged children everywhere to the attention of the more fortunate will never be forgotten.

Some of Danny's more memorable films are *Up in Arms, On the Riviera, The Secret Life of Walter Mitty*, and *Hans Christian Anderson*.

Guess Who's Jewish

And said, "My life was a mish-mosh, then along came M.A.S.H. He was married to a great singing star.

Elliott Goldstein

Elliott Gould

Born April 29, 1928 in Brooklyn, New York to Bernard and Lucille (Raver) Goldstein.

Born to a mother who wanted her son to be in show business, Elliott, anxious to please, took speech, dance, singing and dramatics, and he was only eight years old.

Charles Lowe, his teacher, organized a Vaudeville act which played temples, weddings, hospital groups, and other events in the New York area.

Occasionally, a TV spot came along. The first TV shot brought the change in the name. Goldstein became Gould.

After one year at Columbia University, Elliott quit and took his shot at Broadway, landing a few parts: *Rumple, Say Darlin', Hit the Deck*, and *I Can Get It For You Wholesale*, his first leading role.

Signing with Columbia Studios, Elliott starred in *Bob and Carol and Ted and Alice* (1969), *M.A.S.H.* (1969, his first solid hit), and *Getting Straight* (1970).

In 1963 Gould married Barbra Streisand. It ended amicably in 1971.

Guess Who's Jewish

And said, "If I have to make it that way, I won't go." (She had been offered the easy way to stardom.) She made it on the wings of an infectious laugh.

G. H.

Goldie Hawn

Born November 21, 1945 in Washington, D.C. to a Jewish mother and a "Wasp from Arkansas" father.

After high school Goldie studied drama at American University, danced at the World's Fair and did summer stock around the country.

In 1967 her agent (Art Simon) signed her with the William Morris Agency, who landed her a supporting role in *Good Morning America*, a sit-com on CBS-TV. It flopped, but she didn't.

Her film debut came in 1969 when she co-starred in *Cactus Flower*, after which she starred in *There's a Girl in My Soup* (1970), *Dollars* (1970), *Butterflies Are Free* (1971), *The Sugerland Express* (1974), *The Duchess and the Dirtwater Fox* (1976), *Shampoo* (1975), and *Private Benjamin* (1980).

Guess Who's Jewish

And said, "There's room at the top even for a little boy from Lithuania." A big star in British films.

Larushka Mischa Skikne

Lawrence Harvey

Born October 1, 1928 to Berand and Ella Skikne in Joniskis, Lithuania.

As a young man Larushka moved to Johannesburg, South Africa where he received his education.

After serving in the British Army (discharged in 1946) he entered the Royal Academy of Dramatic Arts in London. Surprisingly, he stayed only three months to join a repertory company obtaining invaluable experience doing a series of great plays of the past.

Romeo and Juliet provided his first important leading role in films, but *Room at the Top* sent him rocketing to stardom. Some other important films he appeared in were *Crusaders* (1954), *The Good Die Young* (1955), *I Am a Camera* (1955), *Four Feathers* (1956), *The Silent Enemy* (1958), *3 Men in a Boat* (1959), *Butterfield 8* (1960), *Expresso Bango* (1960), and *Summer and Smoke* (1961).

Guess Who's Jewish

And said, "If they could see you through my eyes, you wouldn't look Jewish at all." A musical comedy star.

Joel Katz

Joel Grey

Born April 11, 1932 in Cleveland, Ohio to Mickey Katz, a musical star in his own right.

Joel started in show business doing featured acts with his father's touring show and grew up working his routines in Miami Beach hotels, where Eddie Cantor saw him and booked him for his TV show.

Never a shrinking violet, Joel took advantage of the exposure and got himself high-quality bookings in major nightspots around the U.S. as well as London.

Feeling stagnant, he quit the nightclub circuit and opted to study acting in New York. It was the right move to make.

Combining his talents at acting, singing and dancing, he quickly became the second banana in show after show. Then along came *Cabaret* and the part of the M.C. One reporter wrote his performance was among the greatest in American theatre history.

Guess Who's Jewish

And said, "Okay, I'm one-eyed, but that doesn't make me one-dimensional." He proved his point with a wrinkled raincoat.

P. F.

Peter Falk

Born September 26, 1927 in New York City to Michael and Madeline (Hauser) Falk.

At the age of three, Peter Falk had his right eye removed.

After completing high school, followed by college where he was active in dramatics, Peter worked at a number of jobs around the country. In his spare time he acted in plays produced by amateur theatre groups in the cities where he was employed. Still, the idea to become a professional actor had not occurred to him because of "a childish and romanticized idea that ordinary people do not become actors."

It wasn't until he was 27 that the idea was dispelled. In 1956 Peter made his pro debut in *Don Juan* off Broadway.

After a few minor roles in films, his acting prowess was established in a film entitled *Murder, Inc.* in which he portrayed a vicious assassin. A host of other films followed and eventual stardom.

On TV, *Columbo* was his runaway solid hit. The wrinkled raincoat helped.

John Cassavetes once said of Falk, "He's deep. He's gentle. He's two thousand years old. He's somebody everybody falls in love with."

A few of his major films are *Pocketful of Miracles* (1960), *Castle Keep* (1969), *Murder by Death* (1976), and *The Cheap Detective* (1978).

Guess Who's Jewish

And rolled the dice of life and they came up "Little Joe." With him it's one bonanza after another.

Eugene Orowitz

Michael Landon

Born October 31, 1936 in Forest Hills, New York.
A high school champion javelin hurler grad-
uates and goes the multi-occupation route. Process
server, car washer, waiter and railroad worker.
While unloading freight cars he meets another
drifter who is giving the *acting game* a shot, re-
hearsing a scene to get in the Warner Brothers
acting school. He decides to join in the fun and
much to his surprise, learns that he has a raw
talent for dramatics.

Combining that with his strong good looks, he
soon is landing small roles on major TV productions. On a roll, Michael is noticed by a producer
about to cast a new TV western, *Bonanza*. The role
came up Little Joe and lasted fourteen years. But
now, what to do? The ratings are down! Simple.
Join the *Little House On The Prairie* production and
ride out another "Bonanza."

Guess Who's Jewish

And said, "I'll take romance," and put his money where his mouth is. A great jazz musician.

Arthur Arshawsky

Artie Shaw

Born May 23, 1910 in New York City.

Artie was one of the top musicians of his day and yet curiously did not commit his life to jazz. By the time he was 40 years old, music for the most part was behind him. He had turned to writing.

In 1952, he wrote his autobiography, *The Trouble with Cinderella*. Nineteen sixty-five brought the book *I Love You, I Hate You, Drop Dead*. Then he wrote *Variations on a Theme*, which revolved around a subject Shaw knew as well as any man alive, *Grounds for Divorce in Marriage*.

Artie's collection of wives is legendary: Margaret Allen, Lana Turner, Elizabeth Kern, Ava Gardner, Kathleen Winsor, Doris Dowling, and Evelyn Keyes.

Clara Bow had "it." So did Artie. Ask the ladies.

Guess Who's Jewish

And ended up dead on a hook because he started "Lookin' out for Terry (in an Academy Award-winning film)." He had a Charles Laughton-like career.

R. S.

Rod Steiger

Born April 14, 1925 in Westhampton, Long Island.

Steiger received his actor's training at the Actor's Studio.

Cast as the villain, the tough guy, the bigot, he rarely ended up with the girl.

He is a brilliant craftsman and never showed off that fantastic attention to detail better than in *In The Heat of the Night*, for which he won an Oscar.

I'll always remember him as Charlie, Brando's big brother in *On the Waterfront*.

Some of his more important films were *On the Waterfront* (1954), *Jubal* (1956), *Al Capone* (1959), *The Big Knife* (1955), *The Pawnbroker* (1965), and *In the Heat of the Night* (1967).

Guess Who's Jewish

And said, "I have a thing with the camera." Who could argue? She's a young actress whose sexuality is burning up the screen.

D. W.

Debra Winger

Born in 1955 in Cleveland, Ohio.

She has a father who distributes Kosher food and a mother who used to manage offices. Debra left the family fold at sixteen and attacked life by moving to a kibbutz in Israel. But, ambition was smoldering beneath the surface and took control within a year when Debra left Israel and began making TV commercials upon her return to the U.S. It wasn't long before she cracked the movie business doing small roles and ended up as Wonder Woman's kid sister on TV.

Major motion pictures followed: *Urban Cowboy, An Officer and a Gentleman, Cannery Row,* and *Terms of Endearment.*

Early in life she visualized herself a star. So often we get what we visualize.

Guess Who's Jewish

And said, "My father got a 'quarter,' but I want the whole pie." She got it. An interviewer with style.

B. W.

Barbara Walters

Born September 25, 1931 in Boston, Massachu-
setts to Lou and Dena Walters.

Barbara finished her collegiate activities at
Lawrence College in Bronxville, New York. Simultaneously she was finished with any ideas of teaching or acting. Writing and newscasting were upper-
most in her mind.

She rapidly landed a job with NBC's television
affiliate, WRCA. Restlessly moving on to CBS and
again to a public relations firm (she was there
several years) Barbara seized the opportunity to
write for the *Dave Garroway Show (The Today
Show)* when a slot opened up.

The show featured the "Today Girl" who was
used mainly to pretty up the set. In time, Barbara
landed the Today Girl spot and history was in the
making. She became a first-rate incisive interviewer who managed to get to personalities who
were unapproachable by other TV people.

They call her the Million Dollar Personality. I
call her a person who knows love and successfully
communicates that image, and her rewards have
come because of it.

Guess Who's Jewish

And said, "For personal gain, when questioning people, you must get very personal." He gained and gained and gained.

Myron W.

Mike Wallace

Born May 9, 1918 to Frank and Zina (Scharf-man) Wallace.

Mike entered the University of Michigan in 1935 intending to become a teacher. But a chance job as a radio announcer on the University Radio Station turned his head and sent him toward a show business career.

Graduating in 1939 he found himself in Detroit, Michigan doing acting parts on popular adventure series such as *The Lone Ranger* and the *Green Hornet*. The announcing yen was still very much in his heart.

In and out of the Navy by 1946 he went on to compile an admirable list of credits on television: "Famous Names" (he was the moderator), "Curtain Time," "Fact and Fiction," and "Sky King."

Then in the 1950s Mike hosted numerous TV shows and finally landed in the news department on the Dumont Network.

It was in 1957 that the network sought a man to host a controversial TV interview show and the "Mike Wallace Interview" was born. The "hot seat" had found its way to the TV screen.

After the interview show had run its course, Mike, as hot as the hot seat, landed on "60 Minutes," one of the most successful shows of its kind in history.

Guess Who's Jewish

And said, "I kid you not, dancin's all I got." A superb choreographer.

Milton Greenwald

Michael Kidd

Born August 12, 1919 in New York City to Abraham and Lillian Greenwald.

How does a copy boy at the New York *Daily News* become one of the top national choreographers? Easy! Dance, dance, dance. And then dance some more.

His debut as a dancer was at the Manhattan Opera House. Later he fulfilled a personal dream of dancing at the Chicago Opera House and the Ballet Theatre.

He was choreographer for such great shows as *Guys and Dolls, Finian's Rainbow, Lil' Abner,* and *Destiny Rides Again.*

Guess Who's Jewish

And said, "I wish I could read the comics to the children like one of the greats before me, but these days children are concerned with computers and break dancing."

E. K.

Edward Irving Koch

*Born December 12, 1924 in New York City to
Louis and Joyce Koch.*

From the age of nine he was a person to be
reckoned with. The "mensch" whose first job was
working in a checkroom and followed by the usual
amount of widely varying occupations.

Following his discharge from the Army (three
years) he entered NYU Law School and obtained a
degree in law. In 1949 he was admitted to the Bar.

But practicing law wasn't enough. Politics had
reared its ugly head and Ed jumped into the political ring emerging as the standard bearer of the
New York Reform Movement (1966).

He was the first Democrat in 35 years to be
elected to the City Council of Manhattan's Second
District, after which he was elected to the U.S.
House of Representatives, being re-elected four
times.

His record in the House spoke for itself and
aided him when running for Mayor of New York,
being elected on November 8, 1977, an office he
holds at this writing.

Guess Who's Jewish

And said, "I first appeared on TV for 64,000 reasons." A talk show psychologist.

Joyce Bauer

Joyce Brothers

Born 1927 to Morris and Estelle (Rappaport) Bauer.

She is a person who sets high goals for herself and even as a child, achievement was not a stranger to her.

Bauer became Brothers when she married Milton Brothers in 1949.

After obtaining a degree in psychology at Cornell University she took her advanced work at Columbia in New York City.

Why she had such an intense interest in boxing is anybody's guess, but boxing was her category when she appeared on the "$64,000 Question" TV show. Answering every question fired at her, she captured the ultimate prize—$64,000, and gained herself a national reputation.

Remaining on TV she became co-host of "Sports Showcase" and more importantly, was seen as a guest on many of the top-rated talk shows.

Intimate talk of sex became an important portion of her advice offered to the TV public as she expanded her horizons to human relations.

Radio, TV and a syndicated column that appears in 300 newspapers across the nation occupy most of her time at this writing.

Only five feet tall and weighing only 100 lbs., Dr. Brothers was once described as a "towering dynamo" who is more at ease in front of an audience of thousands than in the intimate setting of her living room.

Guess Who's Jewish

And said, "My advice to you is to ask Dear Abby."

Esther Friedman

Ann Landers

Born July 4, 1918 to Abe and Becky Friedman in Sioux City, Iowa.

Eppie, as she was nicknamed shortly after birth, was born just ahead of her identical twin, "Popo."

Twins they were born and twins they remained. Going their way inseparably, as they thought alike on most subjects and generally operated as a pair. Even to the point of announcing their engagements to be married on the same day.

Longing to belong and failing to, Eppie just "knew" she had a "calling" and *by no coincidence* called the Chicago *Sun Times* in 1955 to apply for a job, helping "Ann Landers" answer her mail, unaware that Ruth Crowley (Ann Landers) had died suddenly that week, putting the syndicated column up for grabs.

The *Sun Times* decided to hold a competition to decide who would take over the column and Eppie Friedman won. Her "calling" had materialized. Her new career was launched.

So, one of the twins had opted for a career in advice. Predictably the other was soon to follow. Popo became Abigail Van Buren, giving advice in her "Dear Abby" column. Both careers are still flourishing.

Guess Who's Jewish

And said, "After I die—I shall return." He didn't.

**Erich
Weiss**

Harry Houdini

Born in 1874 in Budapest, Hungary. Died in 1926.

Harry, to this day, is known as the greatest escape artist of all time.

The man spent his life placing it on the line. His excapes from underwater chains are legendary. No strait jacket ever held him and handcuffs were laughable to him. But, how do you get out of an escape-proof jail? Houdini did it. And he did it within time limits, with style.

His death came as a result of a blow to the stomach by a college boxing champion who had read of his ability to take a punch in that region of the body. However, Harry was taken by surprise and had no time to ready himself for the four blows that were struck. He died of stomach problems six months later. Houdini had often boasted that after his death he would communicate with the living. He was never heard from.

Guess Who's Jewish

And in his writings stated, "I was sexually aroused by seeing my mother naked." A dissector of dreams.

S. F.

Sigmund Freud

Born May 6, 1856 in Freiberg, Moravia (Czecho-
slovakia). Died September 23, 1939.

He spent his life re-interpreting the nature of
the human psyche.

For years his concepts were accepted as established facts only to be discarded, or at least diluted,
in modern day psychology.

But, the power of his name remains even to this
day. His long list of publications include *The Ego
and the ID; The Future of an Illusion; The Interpre-
tation of Dreams; Inhibitions, Symptoms and Anx-
ieties;* and *Civilization and Its Discontents.*

Guess Who's Jewish

And said, "Human activity is essentially a struggle with nature. The struggle to furnish man the means of satisfying his needs. Drink, food, and clothing." Freud might have disagreed.

K. M.

Karl Marx

Born May 5, 1818 to Heinrich Marx, a lawyer, and Henrietta Pressburg of Holland.

He led a life of self-sacrifice, joining organizations dedicated to the betterment of man.

In 1842 he turned to journalism, writing editorials on social and economic issues.

A year later Marx married, moved to Paris and wrote incendiary articles which got him expelled from France. In 1848 he wrote *The Communist Manifesto*, and in 1847 *Das Kapital*. His influence on the political state of the world is still apparent.

Guess Who's Jewish

And said, "Give me Bolshevism or give me death." He got both.

Lev D. Bronstein

Leon Trotsky

Born November 7, 1879 in Yanovka, Ukraine.
A lifelong revolutionary, he met and joined Lenin in London where he joined the Russian Social-Democratic Worker's Party. He later broke with Lenin then reunited after the February Revolution, in which the Imperial Government of Russia was overthrown. It was Trotsky who organized the seizure of power by the Bolsheviks.

When Lenin died, Stalin won the struggle to seize power. Thousands were executed. Trotsky was exiled and shortly after, assassinated on August 20, 1940.

PART II

Would You Believe?

Over the last 500 years the Jews have accounted for only ⅓ of 1% of total world population. And yet, see if you can guess the names of the following people who have made a significant impact on history...

1. The formula providing the human race with the opportunity to take its greatest leap forward in scientific history was devised by _____.

2. The two people who dealt a death blow to polio were _____.

3. It was _____ who guided the gigantic Sears and Roebuck Corporation to its present status as "king of retailers."

4. The awe-inspiring DuPont Company is chaired by _____.

5. The greatest swimmer of all time is _____.

6. One of the greatest quarterbacks in pro football (Chicago Bears) history was _____.

7. One of the greatest pitchers in baseball history was _____.

8. Incredible as it may seem, the first man to ever be paid to play baseball was _____.

101

1. The celebrated **Albert Einstein** (E = MC²)
2. **Dr. Albert E. Sabin** and **Dr. Jonas Salk**
3. **Julius Rosenwald**
4. **Irving Shapiro**
5. **Mark Spitz**
6. **Sid Luckman**
7. **Sandy Koufax**
8. **Lipman E. Pike**

9. The man who brought jeans (Levis) into the prominence they enjoy was _____.

10. The outstanding "Lord of the Underworld" was _____.

11. A Jewish prime minister of France was _____.

12. A Jewish prime minister of Great Britain was _____.

13. One of the greatest chess players of all time is _____.

14. The creators of Superman were _____.

15. The man who formed the Harlem Globetrotters was _____.

16. _____ was the first non-Mormon Governor of Utah.

17. In 1956-57 and 1961-62, there was a Jewish Mayor of Dublin, Ireland called _____.

18. _____ was a Pope who was a descendant of Jews who adopted Christianity.

19. A KGB agent in Cairo, Egypt was a Jew, who later went to Israel, called _____.

20. Four Jewish winners of the Congressional Medal of Honor during the Civil War were _____.

21. Two pilots for the Soviet Union who became heroes were Jewish women called _____.

22. _____ was a Jewish admiral in the Italian Navy and Chief of Intelligence (in the 1930s).

23. The commander of Fort Leavenworth during frontier days was _____.

24. Two Jewish Congressional Medal of Honor winners during World War II were _____.

25. There was a Jewish Miss America named _____.

9. Levi Strauss
10. Meyer Lansky
11. Leon Blum
12. Benjamin Disraeli
13. Bobby Fischer (though he converted to Christianity)
14. Jerry Seigal and Joe Schuster
15. Abe Saperstein
16. Simon Bamberger
17. Robert Briscoe
18. Pope Innocent II (1130-1143)
19. Joseph Rosenthal
20. Henry Heller, Abraham Cohn, Benjamin Levy, and David O'Branski
21. Polina Gelman and Lila Litvak
22. Augusto Capon
23. Reuben E. Hershfield
24. Charles W. Hoffman and Philip C. Katz
25. Bess Myerson

26. A Jewish Miss Universe in 1976 was _____.

27. The man who killed Lee Harvey Oswald was _____.

28. The welterweight champion of the world (1915-1919) was _____.

29. The founder of Gimbels Department Store as well as Saks Fifth Avenue was _____.

30. "The Father of Impressionism" was _____.

31. The legendary actress of the early stage was _____ (1844-1923).

32. The developer of psychoanalysis was _____.

33. The physicist in charge of construction of the first atomic bomb was _____.

34. One of the most celebrated attorneys of all time was _____.

35. The Jewish prime minister of Italy in 1910 was _____.

36. A great justice of the early Supreme Court was _____.

37. Two Jews, _____, were among the founders of the New York Stock Exchange.

38. The man who invented a microphone which made possible the invention of the telephone and radio was _____.

39. The head of the Columbia Broadcasting Company was _____.

40. _____, the great explorer, is thought to be a Spanish Jew by some historians. It is documented that he was financially aided by influential Spanish Jews and among his passengers were Jews of considerate stature.

41. In the year 1841, an English Jew named _____ sailed to Tahiti and married a princess of the Teva clan.

26. **Riva Messinger** from Israel
27. **Jack Ruby (Jacob Rubenstein)**
28. **Ted Lewis** (1893 in London, England, real name **Gershon Mendeloff**)
29. **Adam Gimbel** (1817-1897)
30. **Camille Pissarro**
31. **Sarah Bernhardt**
32. **Sigmund Freud**
33. **Robert J. Oppenheimer** (1904-1967)
34. **Louis Nizer** (born in London, England, and author of *My Life in Court*)
35. **Luigi Luzzati** (1841-1927)
36. **Benjamin Cardozo** (1879-1938)
37. **Benjamin Seixas** and **Ezekiel Hart**
38. **Emil Berliner**
39. **William S. Paley**
40. **Christopher Columbus**
41. **Alexander Salmon**

42. _____ was known as the brains of the Confederacy and was its secretary of state. There were few Southern Jewish gentlemen in those days.

43. Dr. Zhivago was written by _____, a Russian Jew who gave ten years of his life to complete the book. It won him a Nobel Prize in literature.

44. _____ discovered the important principal of "blood types" which made successful blood transfusions possible. He was awarded the Nobel Prize in medicine in 1930. He was an Austrian Jew.

45. The most popular Christmas song of all time, "White Christmas," was written by a Siberian Jew, _____.

46. The most popular Easter song ever written, "Easter Parade," was written by _____.

47. The Oscar winner for Best Actor in 1977 *(Goodbye Girl)* was _____, a Brooklyn-born Jew.

48. A great all time auto racing driver was _____.

49. The creator of L'il Abner is _____.

50. Ellery Queen, one of the top fictional detectives of our time, was created by _____.

51. The author of *Fear of Flying* is _____, a New York City-born Jew.

52. _____, a Jew born in Brooklyn, invented the phrase "Catch 22."

53. Name ten famous Jewish songwriters.

54. Name eight famous Jewish singing stars.

55. Two Jews, amid all the rest of their accomplishments, have even managed to reach outer space. They are _____.

42. Judah P. Benjamin
43. Boris Pasternak
44. Karl Landsteiner
45. Irving Berlin
46. Irving Berlin
47. Richard Dreyfus
48. Mauri Rose
49. Al Capp (Alfred Caplin)
50. Daniel Nathan and Manford Lepofsky
51. Erica Jong
52. Joseph Heller
53. Larry Hart   Richard Rodgers
George Gershwin   Jerome Kern
Ira Gershwin   Arthur Lowe
Oscar Hammerstein   Frank Loesser
Arthur Schwartz   Sammy Kahn
54. Barry Manilow   Georgia Gibbs
Tony Martin   Eddie Fisher
Bette Midler   Steve Lawrence
Barbra Streisand   Billy Joel
55. Captain Kirk (William Shatner) and Mr. Spock
(Leonard Nimoy)

56. The trainer of that great thoroughbred Stymie was _____, who hailed from New York and rose to the Turf Hall of Fame. Stymie earned almost $1,000,000.

57. _____, a country only 36 years after its founding, has risen to the fourth most militarily powerful nation in the world.

58. _____, an Orthodox English Jew, was responsible for one of the most strange and most successful counter-espionage exploits of World War II—"Operation Meatball"—placing false documents on a dead body and planting the body on the Spanish Coast. The English hoped that the Spaniards would discover the body and relay the information to the Germans. It worked. The Nazis were fooled on "D" Day.

59. It was a Jew, _____, who helped bring the British Army up to its stature of a respected modern force.

60. The architect of America's first atomic submarine was _____.

61. Our movie industry was almost entirely founded by seven Jews, _____.

62. _____, of the Detroit Tigers, once threatened Babe Ruth's record of 60 home runs in one season. He hit 58. The record was finally broken by Roger Maris, but in a 162-game season.

63. The dynamic pugilist, _____, was Jewish.

64. *Death of a Salesman*, the great award-winning play, was written by _____.

65. The prime minister of France in 1940 was _____, a Portugese Jew whose ancestors migrated to France in the 1300s.

56. Hirsch Jacobs
57. Israel, the Jewish Homeland
58. Ewen Montague
59. Lord Leslie Hope-Bolisha
60. Admiral Hyman Rickover
61. Paramount Pictures —   Adolph Zukor
    Columbia Pictures —   Harry Cohn
    Twentieth Century Fox —   William Fox
    Metro-Goldwyn-Mayer —   Louie B. Mayer
                                 Sam Goldwyn
                                 Marcus Lowe
    Warner Brothers —   Harry Warner
62. Hank Greenberg
63. Benny Leonard
64. Arthur Miller
65. Pierre Mendes-France

66. The man who first measured the speed of light was _____, a 25-year-old Jewish Naval officer who won the Nobel Prize.

67. _____, a German Jew, was one of the discoverers of penicillin. He received a Nobel Prize in 1945.

68. As early as 1654, _____ Jews landed in New Amsterdam to become the first Jewish community in America.

69. "Rhapsody in Blue," clearly one of the finest musical compositions of the 20th century, was composed by the New York City-born _____.

70. _____ of the gigantic beauty products empire is Jewish.

71. The Maidenform Company was founded by _____.

72. A pilot in the Russian Air Force gave his life attacking a German warship kamikaze-style. He was _____.

73. A Jew, _____, was on the plane that dropped the bomb on Nagasaki.

74. The beloved Italian mayor of New York, _____, had a Jewish mother.

75. A Polaroid camera was invented by _____.

76. The extremely successful Jewish talk show psychologist is _____.

77. In 1520 _____, a wealthy Jew from Constantinople, was appointed finance minister and master of the mint of Egypt.

78. When Sulieman defeated the Hungarians in the Battle of Mohacs in 1526, the keys of the city were handed to him by a Jew named _____.

66. **Albert Michelson** (1852-1931)
67. **Ernst Boris Chain**
68. 23
69. **George Gershwin**
70. **Vidal Sassoon**
71. **William Rosenthal**
72. **Ilya Katonin**
73. **Jacob Besser**
74. **Fiorello LaGuardia**
75. **Edward Land**

76. **Dr. Joyce Brothers**
77. **Abraham Castro**
78. **Joseph B. Soloman Ashkenazi**

79. Vitamins were first discovered in 1911 by
_____, a Jewish biochemist from Poland.

80. _____, a Russian Jew (1860-1930), discovered
a vaccine to be used to fight cholera and the
Black Plague.

81. _____ was the discoverer of the planet
Uranus in March of 1781.

82. _____ discovered the existence of
electromagnetic waves which led to the
invention of wireless telephone and telegraph.

83. _____ of Germany was the first to build a
satisfactory gas automobile engine.

84. _____ was the man responsible for the
Schick injector razors.

85. _____ had his invention rights sold by his
wife (after his death) to Graf Ferdinand Von
Zeppelin, who later constructed the famous Graf
Zeppelin using Schwartz's plans.

86. _____, a Hungarian Jew, was once known as
the world's best table tennis player.

87. The Jews have their jockey representative,
_____, whose mounts won over
$10,000,000.

88. The Jews also have their bullfighter, _____
(the toreador from Brooklyn), who toured the
Spanish bullring circuit.

89. The quarterback "who never made a mistake" was
_____, the Michigan U football genius. So
said Knute Rochne, and who would know better?

90. The biggest "mouth" in sportscasting history is
_____. I'm one of his biggest fans.

91. The hottest screen director on the screen today is
_____, director of *Jaws*, *Close Encounters
of the Third Kind*, and the fantastic *E.T.*

113

79. Casimir Funk (1884-1967)
80. Waldemar Mordecai Haffkine
81. Sir William Herschel (1738-1822)
82. Heinrich Hertz
83. Seigfried Marcus (1831-1898)
84. Bela Schick
85. David Schwartz (1845-1897)
86. Victor Barna
87. Walter Blum
88. Sidney Franklin
89. Benny Friedman
90. Howard Cosell
91. Steven Spielberg

92. The most famous newspaper gossip columnist and radio newscaster of all time was _____.

93. The chairman of the board and founder of the Diner's Club is _____.

94. The man who provided the inspiration for the Christian religion was _____.

95. The inventor of stainless steel was _____.

96. The first airline passenger to cross the Atlantic was _____.

97. The man who said, "You pay the top 'Vig' and the seats are yours! Dig?" is _____. He is still the leading ticket agent in the Metro New York area (over 40 years).

98. The beatles didn't hit the big time until they switched drummers. The added ingredient that sent them winging was _____ from Liverpool.

99. The two most widely syndicated advice columnists are the twins _____.

92. **Walter Winchell**
93. **Alfred S. Bloomingdale**
94. **Jesus Christ**
95. **Benno Strauss** of Germany
96. **Charles A. Levine**
97. Bamberger's **Harry Chetkin**
98. **Ringo Starr**
99. **Abigail Van Buren**   and   **Ann Landers**
    (Pauline Friedman)   **(Esther Friedman)**
    Dear Abby   Dear Ann

PART III

The Comedians

Those daredevils of the stage who nightly summon up the courage to face an audience which is, en masse, thinking, "Go ahead, make me laugh." And if the comedian does indeed *make them laugh,* he becomes "one" with the audience, reaching heights of euphoria undreamed of. But, if the laughs don't come, the stage is a lonely place and the plunge off the cliff to the abyss below seems bottomless. And what about tomorrow? And tomorrow's tomorrow? Here are a few of those Jewish daredevils...

Don Adams
The "Get Smart" man.
1927—New York City

Joey Adams (Joseph Abramowitz)
Nightclub entertainer, radio personality,
newspaper columnist and president of AGVA.
1911—New York City

Jack Kruschen
Funny, hefty comic actor.
1922—Winnipeg, Manitoba, Canada

Woody Allen
A real sleeper and a reel sleeper.
1936—Brooklyn, New York

Morey Amsterdam
Remember the "Dick Van Dyke Show"?
1914—Chicago, Illinois

Jack Benny
Silence was his greatest asset (along with his
violin).
1894-1974—Chicago, Illinois

Milton Berle
Mr. Television as Uncle Miltie.
1908—New York City

Shelley Berman
Standup comic who achieved wide success.
1926—Chicago, Illinois

Joey Bishop (Joey Gottlieb)
TV talk show host and nightclub comic.
1919—Bronx, New York

Victor Borge (Borge Rosenbaum)
The "One Man" show.
1909—Denmark

David Brenner
Thank God for Johnny Carson.
1945—Philadelphia, Pennsylvania

Mel Brooks (Melvin Kaminsky)
Great comedic actor, director.
1911—Philadelphia, Pennsylvania

Lenny Bruce (Leonard Schneider)
"Informed" comic.
1926-1966—

George Burns (Nathan Birnbaum)
"Burns and Allen" to Oh, God
1896-New York City

Red Buttons (Aaron Chwatt)
Academy Award-winning actor for Sayonara *and television comedian as well as nightclub comic.*
1919-New York City

Sid Caesar
"The Show of Shows"—a super innovative television presentation.
1922—Yonkers, New York

Eddie Cantor (Isador Iskowitch)
Top notch musical comedy star.
1892-1964—New York City

Jack Carter (Jack Chakrin)
One of the better comics still on the scene today.
1923—New York City

Myron Cohen
The ultimate Jewish dialectician.
1902—Grodno, Poland

Al Schacht
"Clown" prince of baseball. A clown in baggy pants.
1892—New York City

Bill Dana (William Szathmary)
Remember "Jose Jimenez"?
1924—Quincy, Massachusetts

Rodney Dangerfield (Jacob Cohen)
Respect seems to elude him.
1921—Babylon, New York

Totie Fields (Sophie Feldman)
One of the top comediennes.
1931-1978—Hartford, Connecticut

Larry Fine
One of the great Three Stooges.
1902-1975—New York City

Phil Foster (Philip Feldman)
A very funny contemporary comic.
1914—Brooklyn, New York

David Frye (David Friedman)
A super impersonator.
1934—Brooklyn, New York

Curly Howard (Jerome Horowitz)
One of the original Three Stooges.
1907-1952—

Moe Howard (Maurice Horowitz)
One of the original Three Stooges.
1897-1975—

Shemp Howard (Samuel Horowitz)
One of the original Three Stooges.
1895-1955)

Milt Kamen
One of the funny TV comics.
1924—Harleyville, New York

Lou Jacobi (Louis Jacobovitch)
Primarily a comic actor.
1913—Toronto, Canada

Stubby Kaye
Funny actor in Guys and Dolls.
1918—

Jack Gilford (Jack Gellman)
A star comic act of merit.
1907—New York City

Bud Flanagan (Weinthrop)
Superb British music hall comic
1896-1968—London, England

Buddy Hackett (Leonard Hacker)
A funny, funny man.
1924—Brooklyn, New York

Marty Ingels
Comic-actor.
1936—Brooklyn, New York

George Jessel
Followed Will Rogers as toastmaster of the United States.
1898-1983—New York City

Gabe Kaplin
The stand-up comedian who hit on TV with "Welcome Back Kotter."
1945—Brooklyn, New York

Danny Kaye
One of the all-time greats.
1913—Brooklyn, New York

Alan King (Irwin Kniberg)
Fine comedian, fine actor.
1924—Brooklyn, New York

Harvey Korman
Standout on Carol Burnett Show with super versatility.
1927—Chicago, Illinois

Bert Lahr (Irving Lahrheim)
The lovable Cowardly Lion in Wizard of Oz.
1895-1967—New York City

Louise Lasser
"Mary Hartman, Mary Hartman."
1942—New York City

Pinky Lee (Pincus Leff)
A funny TV comic.
1916—St. Paul, Minnesota

Jackie Mason
"Remember the finger incident on Ed Sullivan, Mister?"
1931—Sheboygan, Wisconsin

Harvey Lembeck
A funny actor—remember "Stalag 17?"
1923—New York City

Jack E. Leonard
He even "insulted" Don Rickles.
1911-1973

Jerry Lester
Was predecessor of "Tonight Show" on late night TV.
1911—Chicago, Illinois

Sam Levinson
Teacher turned comedian who reminisces.
1914—U.S.S.R.

Jerry Lewis (Joseph Levitch)
1926—Newark, New Jersey

Shari Lewis
TV puppeteer, ever popular.
1934—New York City

Chico Marx (Leonard)
The piano-playing brother.
1891-1961—New York City

Groucho Marx (Julius)
The Lover?
1895-1977—New York City

Zeppo Marx (Herbert)
Actor turned agent.
1901—New York City

Gummo Marx (Milton)
Dropped out early.
1894-1978—New York City

Harpo Marx (Arthur)
"The Mute."
1893-1964—New York City

Elaine May
Joined with Mike Nichols to form a great team.
1932—Philadelphia, Pennsylvania

Jan Murry (Murray Janofsky)
Excellent TV and nightclub performer.
1917—New York City

Howard Morris
A part of the great "Your Show of Shows."
A fine writer.
1919—New York City

Martha Raye
One of the greatest to grace a stage.
1916—Butte, Montana

Fanny Brice
Baby Snooks and Billy Rose.
1881-1951—New York City

Carl Reiner
A great comic writer but also a great performer.
Remember Sid Caesar's "Your Show of Shows?"
1922—Bronx, New York

Don Rickles
The master of the "insult" technique.
1920—New York City

Rob Reiner
A solid smash on "All in the Family."
Son of Carl Reiner.
1946—Bronx, New York

Joan Rivers (Molinsky)
From writer to performer.
1935—New York City

Harry Ritz
One of the great comedy team.
1906—Newark, New Jersey

Al Ritz
One of the great comedy team.
1901-1965—Newark, New Jersey

Jim Ritz
One of the great comedy team.
1903—Newark, New Jersey

Mort Sahl
The satiric social comedian.
1927—Montreal, Canada

Soupy Sales (Milton Hines)
Much of his material is for children.
1925—Franklinton, North Carolina

Peter Sellers
One of the great comic actors of all time.
1925-1982—Southsea, England

Alan Sherman
Rotund comedian—slightly offbeat material.
(My son the Folk Singer.)
1924-1973—New York City

Phil Silvers (Silversmith)
I'll never forget Sergeant Bilko.
1912—Brooklyn, New York

David Steinberg
Contemporary comedian making a name
for himself.
1942—Winnipeg, Canada

Smith & Dale (Joseph Seltzer & Charles Marks)
The classic comedy team.
Seltzer-1884—Marks-1882

Larry Storch
A standout comedian and impressionist.
1925—New York City

Arnold Stang
Remember him on Milton Berle's show?
1925—Chelsea, Massachusetts

Al Schean
The Vaudevillian.
1868-1949—Dornum, Germany

Gene Wilder (Jerome Silberman)
Superb writer and actor in comedy.
1934—Milwaukee, Wisconsin

Henry Winkler
"The Fonz."
1945—New York City

Ed Wynn (Isaiah Leopold)
Classic actor comedian.
1886-1966—Philadelphia, Pennsylvania

Henny Youngman
Hilarious "one liner" comic.
1906—Liverpool, England

Larry Wilde (Wildman)
Joke book author.
1928—Jersey City, New Jersey

Dick Shawn (Schulefand)
A funny man who just missed.
1929—Buffalo, New York

Johnny Wayne
Comic and writer.
1918—Toronto, Canada

Frank Schuster
Canadian comic and writer.
1916—Toronto, Canada

Bea Arthur
A fine comedic actress.
1926—New York City

PART IV

Jewish Sports Stars

(Match the clue to the name.)

___ 1. English Sprinter	A Lenny Rosenbluth
___ 2. "Lost 58"	B Al Davis
___ 3. K Phenom	C Sandy Koufax
___ 4. Yankee Outfielder	D Dick Savitt
___ 5. Two Club Feet	E Benny Friedman
___ 6. Beat the Habit	F Al McCoy
___ 7. Michigan Quarterback	G Harold Maurice Abrahams
___ 8. "How About That?"	
___ 9. Gold Rush of 1972	H Barney Ross
___ 10. Trained Stymie	I Art Heyman
___ 11. Globetrotters	J Ron Blumberg
___ 12. Raider Runner	K Mendy Rudolph
___ 13. 50s Tennis Star	L Hirsch Jacobs
___ 14. Cage Ref Supreme	M Barry Kramer
___ 15. Won Wimbledon	N Johnny Kling
___ 16. Cub Catcher	O Mel Allen
___ 17. Duke Cager	P Herbert Flam
___ 18. "The Horse"	Q Larry Sherry
___ 19. All-Amer. at U. of No. Car.	R Abe Saperstein
___ 20. "The Clown"	S Hank Greenberg
___ 21. Lefty Middleweight Champ	T Mark Spitz
	U Al Schact
___ 22. NYU Cage Great	V Harry Danning

(Answers Start Page 134)

___ 1. World Chess Champ	A Elias Katz
___ 2. Rode 4,383 Winners	B Moe Berg
___ 3. Golf Great	C Al Rosen
___ 4. Colts and Rams	D Walter Blum
___ 5. Twin No-Hitters	E Sid Luckman
___ 6. Cy Young Sportscaster	F Robert Fischer
___ 7. Bear from Columbia	G Benny Leonard
___ 8. Female Kegler	H Art Shamsky
___ 9. Nat Natural	I Michael Epstein
___ 10. Owl Mentor	J Harry Litwak
___ 11. Diamond Squatter	K Dolph Schayes
___ 12. Spy	L Maxie Rosenbloom
___ 13. Nine Years in Majors	M Ken Holtzman
___ 14. Miracle Met	N Abe Attell
___ 15. MVP 1953	O Carrol Rosenbloom
___ 16. All Star NHL	P Sylvia Wene Martin
___ 17. Lightweight Champ	Q Hy Buller
___ 18. Southpaw Lightweight	R Amy Alcott
___ 19. Featherweight Champ	S Norm Sherry
___ 20. Finnish Runner	T Steve Stone
___ 21. Slapsie	U Lew Tendler

(Answers Start Page 137)

_____ 1. Ref Elite   A Tal Brody

_____ 2. Coach Supreme   B Sidney Franklin

_____ 3. Original Celtic   C Red Auerbach

_____ 4. Charger   D Ernie Grunfeld

_____ 5. Panther   E Andrew Cohen

_____ 6. Coached Warriors   F Brian Gottfried

_____ 7. Fashion Bowler   G Ron Mix

_____ 8. Israeli Cager   H Marshall Holman

_____ 9. McGraws Man   I Ruby Goldstein

_____ 10. French Speedster   J Barney Dreyfus

_____ 11. Pirate Owner   K Eddie Gottlieb

_____ 12. Boxing Crusader   L Red Holtzman

_____ 13. Bullfighter   M Schlomo Glickstein

_____ 14. Israeli Net Star   N Randy Grossman

_____ 15. Baseball Giant   O Nat Fleischer

_____ 16. Top 20 Racket Ace   P Barry Asher

_____ 17. Caught for Steelers   Q Julie Heldman

_____ 18. N. Y. Knick   R Marshall Goldberg

_____ 19. Female Tennis Pro   S Nat Holman

_____ 20. Ace Kegler   T Rene Dreyfuss

_____ 21. Coached Knicks   U Sid Gordon

(Answers Start Page 140)

_____ 1. "Kid" A George Stone

_____ 2. Light Heavy Champ B Tom Okker

_____ 3. K. C. Chiefs C Marv Levy

_____ 4. Female Cage Star D Elliott Teltscher

_____ 5. Newark Bowler E Maurice Podoloff

_____ 6. Dutch Tennis Ace F Neal Walk

_____ 7. Baseball's First Pro G Myron Drabowski

_____ 8. Knicks Announcer H Louis Kaplan

_____ 9. NBA Prexy I Edward Reulbach

_____ 10. Double Header Shutouts J Morrie Arnovich

_____ 11. Three-Time Bowler of Year K Nancy Lieberman

_____ 12. Human Backboard L Marty Glickman

_____ 13. "Silent" M Larry Brown

_____ 14. Up to 8th in Tennis N Mark Roth

_____ 15. Up to 7th in Tennis O Norm Grekin

_____ 16. So-So Ball Player P Mort Lindsay

_____ 17. ABA, NBA Coach Q Harold Solomon

_____ 18. U. of Fla. to NBA R Battling Levinsky

_____ 19. '48 NBA Top Scorer S Max Zaslovsky

_____ 20. "Moe" T Brian Teacher

_____ 21. LaSalle Standout U Lipman Pike

(Answers Start Page 144)

Answers For Page 130

1. **G** HAROLD MAURICE ABRAHAMS—*English Sprinter*
(1899-1978)
The great film *Chariots of Fire* told his story. A world-class sprinter, he used his speed as an answer to the anti-semitism rampant in English society early in the 20th century.

2. **S** HANK GREENBERG—*"Lost 58" (b. 1911)*
While playing for the Detroit Tigers in the American league, Hank hit (lost) 58 home runs during the 1938 season. Up to that time no one had even come close to Babe Ruth's record of 60. Roger Maris later hit 61 in a 162-game season.

3. **C** SANDY KOUFAX—*K Phenom* (b. 1935)
He was the youngest player ever admitted to the Baseball Hall of Fame. During his career he struck out (K'd) 2,396 batters. Sandy was fast, to say the least.

4. **J** RON BLUMBERG—*Yankee Outfielder* (b. 1948)
Ron played for the N. Y. Yankees most of his baseball career, finishing with the Chicago White Sox. Prone to injury, the promise of a great career never materialized. However, he did have some outstanding years.

5. **Q** LARRY SHERRY—*Two Club Feet* (b. 1935)
Born with two club feet, Larry amazingly overcame the handicap to play high school baseball and basketball. It was in baseball that he made the Majors where he played for the Los Angeles Dodgers as well as the Tigers, Astros and Angels. You'd have to say Larry Sherry had "True Grit."

6. **H** BARNEY ROSS—*Beat the Habit* (1909-1967)
A silver star winner in WW II, he took morphine to ease the pain of malaria he had picked up in the South Pacific. Sadly, Barney became addicted and it was to take its toll in his personal life. Finally, he beat the habit by spending four months in a narcotics rehab center in Lexington, Kentucky. Barnet David Rosofsky was the first fighter to hold the Lightweight and Welterweight titles simultaneously.

7. E   BENNY FRIEDMAN—*Michigan Quarterback* (1905-1982)
Benny was the starting quarterback on the 1925
Michigan U. football team. He was named All-American
after enjoying a memorable season. 1926 was a repeat
performance and another All-American selection.

8. O   MEL ALLEN (Melvin Israel)—*"How About That"* (b. 1913)
The voice of the Yankees for many years. I've always
considered Mel one of the premier sportscasters in the
business. *How about that?*

9. T   MARK SPITZ—*Gold Rush of 1972* (b. 1950)
Mark won seven gold medals winning all seven events
he entered in the 1972 Olympics. Amazingly, he broke
the world record in all seven events. One of the greatest
achievements in sports history.

10. L   HIRSCH JACOBS—*Trained Stymie* (1904-1970)
One of the great American race horse trainers, his
mounts won 3,569 races. Stymie, winner of over
$900,000, a world record, was trained by Hirsch. Stymie
is considered among the greatest race horses of all time.

11. R   ABE SAPERSTEIN—*The Harlem Globetrotters* (1903-1966)
The Harlem Globetrotters were created, coached and
owned by Abe. They are still the most incredible sports
aggregation to ever grace the sports scene. Founded in
1927, the Globetrotters have entertained the world for 57
years.

12. B   AL DAVIS—*Raider Runner* (b. 1929)
Al built the Oakland Raiders into a powerful football
force. He truly *runs the raiders*, taking them to three
Super Bowls, 1977, 1981, and 1984.

13. P   HERBERT FLAM—*50s Tennis Star* (b. 1928)
Was one of the top tennis players in the world during
the 1950s. In 1952 he was ranked 10th in the world.

14. K   MENDY RUDOLPH—*Cage Ref Supreme* (b. 1928)
Whenever the hot stove league convenes Mendy's
name invariably emerges. He is considered one of the
most outstanding basketball referees of all time.

15. **D** DICK SAVITT—*Won Wimbledon* (b. 1927)
Dick is the only Jewish tennis player to ever win at
Wimbledon. He won in 1951 when he was ranked 10th in
the world. Herb Flam, another Jewish net star was
defeated by Savitt in the semi-finals of that tournament.

16. **N** JOHNNY KLING (Kline)—*Cub Catcher* (1875-1947)
Due to the more pronounced anti-semitic feeling
existing in America at the turn of the century, Kline
changed his name to Kling. Baseball men rate him as
one of the most talented receivers of all time. Kling was
the first catcher to stand directly behind the batter.

17. **I** ART HEYMAN—*Duke Cager* (b. 1942)
A three-time All-American at Duke University—1961,
1962, 1963—he went on to play seven years in the pro
ranks. In 1963 he was College Player of the Year.

18. **V** HARRY DANNING—*"The Horse"* (b. 1911)
Nicknamed "The Horse," Harry played nine years with
the N. Y. Giants. His lifetime average was .285 but he did
hit over .300 on three separate occasions. He made the
All-Star Team in 1939, 1940 and 1941.

19. **A** LENNY ROSENBLUTH—*All-American at U. No. Car.* (b.
1933)
Was an All-American at the University of North Carolina
in 1955, 1956 and 1957. Later, he coached at Coral Gables
High School in Miami, Florida. I remember his classic
battles with Key West High School's team who were
coached by Dave Fedor.

20. **U** AL SCHACT—*"The Clown"* (b. 1892)
Made his mark as the "Clown Prince of Baseball." Prior
to clowning he had a brief career as a pitcher in the
Majors.

21. **F** AL MCCOY—*Lefty Middleweight Champ* (b. 1894)
Born Al Rudolph, he was middleweight champion of the
world and held the title three years.

22. **M** BARRY KRAMER—*NYU Cage Great* (b. 1942)
A great star with NYU in the 1960s. Barry was on the All-
American Basketball team in 1963, 1964.

Answers For Page 131

1. **F** ROBERT (Bobby) FISCHER—*World Chess Champ* (b. 1943)
   Although Bobby converted to Christianity, I felt compelled to include him in *Guess Who's Jewish*. I guess it goes like this—"Once a Jew, Always a Jew." Bobby Fischer is a world-renowned chess player. He was born to compete at chess. At 15, he was International Grandmaster.

2. **D** WALTER BLUM—*Rode 4,383 Winners* (b. 1934)
   Trotted to the winner's circle 4,383 times. Riding during the 1950s and 1960s he was genuinely one of America's greatest jockeys.

3. **R** AMY ALCOTT—*Golf Great* (b. 1956)
   Currently one of the leading money winners on the tour, she was Rookie of the Year in 1975-1976.

4. **O** CARROL ROSENBLOOM—*Colts and Rams* (1908-1978)
   The flamboyant owner of the Baltimore Colts who later switched to the L. A. Rams.

5. **M** KEN HOLTZMAN—*Twin No-Hitters* (b. 1945)
   After pitching two no-hitters for the Chicago Cubs, the Cubs true to their policy of trading away the money seekers, let Holtzman go to the Oakland Athletics. Holtzman flourished there. He was on the team that won three straight World Series. His lifetime record was 174-150. In recent years the Cubs have changed their ways.

6. **T** STEVE STONE—*Cy Young Sportscaster* (b. 1947)
   Another in the parade of players that got away from the Chicago Cubs. He stayed three years and ended up with the Baltimore Orioles where he won a Cy Young Award. Steve is now a fledgling sports announcer and doing very well.

7. **E** SID LUCKMAN—*Bear from Columbia* (b. 1916)
   When the great quarterbacks are discussed, Sid Luckman's name is always brought up as being one of the best to ever play football. He was All-American at Columbia under Coach Lou Little and then signed with George Halas and the Chicago Bears. Bear fans were

luckier than Cub fans. Luckman played his entire career with Chicago.

8. **P** SYLVIA WENE MARTIN—*Female Kegler* (b. 1930)
One of the greatest women bowlers of all time, Sylvia achieved Bowler of the Year awards in 1955 and 1960. She had three perfect games to her credit. 900 is a lot of pins in three games.

9. **K** DOLPH SCHAYES—*Nat Natural* (b. 1928)
The great all-around forward for the Syracuse Nationals entry in the National Basketball Association, Dolph retired as the all-time scoring leader (19,249 points). 6,979 were free throws.

10. **J** HARRY LITWAK—*Owl Mentor* (b. 1907)
The coach of the Temple Owls for over 20 years. Prior to being head coach, Harry was freshman coach for another 20 years. That's over 40 years at Temple, something worth cheering about.

11. **S** NORM SHERRY—*Diamond Squatter* (b. 1931)
Brother of Larry Sherry, Norm was roommate of Sandy Koufax, who credits him with advice that helped turn Koufax into the great pitcher he became. Norm was a catcher with the Dodgers at that time.

12. **B** MOE BERG—*Spy* (1902-1972)
Moe graduated Princeton University in 1923 and went on to the Major Leagues where he became a premier catcher with the Chicago White Sox and Cleveland Indians. Incredibly, he left baseball to become a counter-intelligence agent for the United States during World War II.

13. **I** MICHAEL EPSTEIN—*Nine Years in Majors* (b. 1943)
A Major League baseball player who played nine years and best distinguished himself when he tied the record by hitting four home runs in four successive times at bat. Mike played for a variety of teams as most journeymen do.

14. **H** ART SHAMSKY—*Miracle Met* (b. 1941)
Baseball player turned agent and broadcaster. Shamsky's claim to fame is playing for the "Miracle Mets" of 1969.

15. **C** AL ROSEN—*MVP 1953* (b. 1925)
One of the great third basemen who have played for the Cleveland Indians (1947-1956). Al Rosen won the Most Valuable Player Award in 1953. From 1950-1954, Al had over 100 RBI's each season.

16. **Q** HY BULLER—*All Star NHL* (b. 1926)
He was a defenseman for the N. Y. Rangers and Detroit Red Wings and once made the second-team All Stars.

17. **G** BENNY LEONARD—*Lightweight Champ* (1896-1947)
Real name Benjamin Leiner. Leonard is considered to be the best Jewish sports figure of all time.

18. **U** LEW TENDLER—*Southpaw Lightweight* (b. 1898)
The southpaw lightweight who was often referred to as the best lefthanded lightweight of all time. Bad timing prevented Tendler from wearing the crown, having come along during Benny Leonard's tenure.

19. **N** ABE ATTELL—*Featherweight Champ* (1884-1969)
His real name was Albert Knochr. He was World Featherweight champ from 1902-1912. Damon Runyan called him one of the top five boxers of all time. He was a solid hitter who stood only 5'4" and weighed 122 pounds.

20. **A** ELIAS KATZ—*Finnish Runner* (1901-1947)
Elias qualified for the 1924 Olympics. He won a Gold Medal as well as a Silver Medal. While preparing to enter the 1928 games, a foot problem prevented his participation.

21. **L** MAXIE ROSENBLOOM—*Slapsie* (1904-1976)
Hitting his opponents with an open glove earned Max the nickname of "Slapsie." With a style like that it's hard to imagine him holding the light heavyweight crown. But, hold it he did, defeating Jimmy Slattery in 15 rounds in Buffalo, N. Y. on June 25, 1930.

Answers For Page 132

1. **I** RUBY GOLDSTEIN—*Ref Elite* (b. 1907)
Best known as a referee, but a boxer earlier in his
career, Ruby managed to win 50 fights competing in the
lightweight division. He lost only five.

2. **C** RED AUERBACH—*Coach Supreme* (b. 1918)
Red must be ranked among the greatest basketball
coaches of all time as well as being tops among General
Managers in the pro ranks. The Boston Celtics in the 50s,
60s, 70s and 80s have been as formidable as any sports
team anywhere at any time. Red was with them all the
way.

3. **S** NAT HOLMAN—*Original Celtic* (b. 1896)
One of the greatest basketball players of all time, who
played for the *original Celtics*, then went on to become a
top notch coach at CCNY.

4. **G** RON MIX—*Charger* (b. 1938)
Developed into one of the greatest offensive tackles of
all time. Ron is in the San Diego Chargers Hall of Fame.
He was All-Pro several times.

5. **R** MARSHALL GOLDBERG—*Panther* (b. 1918)
First team All American in 1937 and 1938. While playing
for University of Pittsburgh Panthers, Marshall went on
to a successful career with the Chicago Cardinals.

6. **K** EDDIE GOTTLIEB—*Coached Warriors* (1900-1979)
Instrumental in founding the National Basketball
Association, Eddie was Head Coach of the Philadelphia
Warriors from 1947-1956. He is in the Basketball Hall of
Fame.

7. **P** BARRY ASHER—*Fashion Bowler* (b. 1946)
Barry was known as the fashion plate of bowling. He
was also called "the best unknown bowler in the
country." In 1976 he won 10 titles on tour, only the 15th
bowler in history to accomplish that feat.

8. **A** TAL BRODY—*Israeli Cager* (b. 1943)
Tal was born in Trenton, New Jersey, received a degree
from the University of Illinois and migrated to Israel

where he starred on the basketball court for the Israelis. He remained in Israel and helped build the basketball program as well as other sports programs.

9. **E** ANDREW COHEN—*McGraw's Man* (b. 1904)
Andrew was chosen by John McGraw to be the Jewish player the New York fans longed for. However, his career was a short one. Still, he did manage a lifetime batting average of .281.

10. **T** RENE DREYFUSS—*French Speedster* (b. 1905)
The French racing driver who won 36 races over a 16-year span (1924-1940). He had the distinction of serving in both the French and American armies during World War II.

11. **J** BARNEY DREYFUS—*Pirate Owner* (1865-1932)
They call him the "Father" of the World Series, having arranged a meeting on the field of the American League Champions, the Boston Pilgrims and his own Pittsburgh Pirates, the National League champs. Barney was the owner of the Pirates from 1900-1932.

12. **O** NAT FLEISCHER—*Boxing Crusader* (1887-1972)
He was the founder and editor of *Ring Magazine*. His passion was boxing as early as his pre-teen years. Later, he became boxing's greatest "out of the ring" champion. As editor, sportswriter, promoter, referee, Nat fought courageously to clean up boxing in order to present to the public an unblemished sport that would merit their confidence. Generally speaking, he failed. Boxing still remains, as far as integrity is concerned, very suspect.

13. **B** SIDNEY FRANKLIN—*Bullfighter* (1903-1976)
Real name, Frumkin. He was known as the first Jewish bullfighter (not documented) and became one of the top matadors of Spain. His fame spread through Portugal, Mexico, as well as South America. And, as in the case in all walks of life, the occupational hazard reared its ugly head. Sidney was gored by a bull and was forced to retire in 1930.

14. **M** SCHLOMO GLICKSTEIN—*Israeli Net Star* (b. 1958)
The Israeli tennis slickster who reached a ranking of 22nd in the ATP listings of 1982. By his own admission,

Schlomo was never among the tennis elite. But, despite his modesty, he did defeat many of the top players at one time or another.

15. **U** SID GORDON—*Baseball Giant* (1918-1975)
Sid played 13 years in the Major Leagues with the New York Giants and Boston Braves. The popular outfielder hit 202 home runs and drove in over 800 runs during a highly respectable career.

16. **F** BRIAN GOTTFRIED—*Top 20 Racket Ace* (b. 1952)
Brian is still today a viable force in world tennis. His highest ranking was achieved in 1976 when he was 10th in the ATP rankings. I don't feel he ever reached his full potential, but it wasn't for lack of trying.

17. **N** RANDY GROSSMAN—*Caught for Steelers* (b. 1952)
All-American at Temple U, he never achieved All-Star status in the pros. But, he did achieve more than a measure of respectability while helping the Pittsburgh Steelers win the 1978 Super Bowl, catching three passes in that game. The "Rabbi," as he was dubbed by the other Steelers, had proved his point.

18. **D** ERNIE GRUNFELD—*N. Y. Knick* (b. 1955)
In 1977 Ernie started his pro basketball career with the Milwaukee Bucks. Currently he is in the supporting cast of the N. Y. Knicks.

19. **Q** JULIE HELDMAN—*Female Tennis Pro* (b. 1945)
You might ask, "Who is Julie Heldman?" I'll tell you. One of the top female tennis players on the tour during the 1960s. She was a baseline player who won with her "head"while lacking the raw talent some others possessed.

20. **H** MARSHALL HOLMAN—*Ace Kegler* (b. 1954)
A bowler who reached super stardom on the lanes earning over $100,000 in one year. Not an easy task in bowling, as anyone on the tour will readily attest.

21. **L** RED HOLTZMAN—*Coached Knicks* (b. 1920)
He was an All-American at CCNY, and an all league player in the NBA. Basketball was his game and as player, coach and scout he made his presence felt. The New York Knicks hired Red as coach in 1967. In only two years he led them to the world title. He was chosen NBA Coach of the Year in 1970.

Answers For Page 133

1. **H** LOUIS KAPLAN—*"Kid"* (1902-1970)
   Born Gershon Hendeloff. On the boxing scene he was
   ranked 10th on the all-time featherweight listings. In
   1925 an elimination tournament was held to determine
   who would be the new champion. The title had been
   vacated by Johnny Dundee. "Kid" won that elimination.
   He was then featherweight champion of the world.

2. **R** BATTLING LEVINSKY—*Light Heavy Champ* (1891-1949)
   Born Barney Lebrowitz. Light heavy champion from 1916-
   1920, Levinsky became a boxing instructor during World
   War II. He returned to boxing after receiving his
   discharge, but the old magic was gone. Jack Dempsey,
   on his way to the top, knocked him out in 1918.

3. **C** MARV LEVY—*K. C. Chiefs* (b. 1928)
   Marv tried coaching in Canada first, being head coach of
   the Montreal Alouettes for five years. Prior to that he
   had been an assistant coach in the NFL. But, it was at
   Kansas City he achieved his most notable feats,
   coaching the K. C. Chiefs to a 31-42 record from 1978-1982.

4. **K** NANCY LIEBERMAN—*Female Cage Star* (b. 1958)
   She was a basketball super star at Old Dominion
   University, who recruited her in 1976, snatching her
   away from 75 other colleges. Later, she was to repeat
   her performance as a pro super star.

5. **P** MORT LINDSAY—*Newark Bowler* (1888-1969)
   He came out of Newark, N. J. to show the country that
   even Newarkers can bowl with the best. Eleven men
   were originally chosen for the Bowling Hall of Fame.
   Mort was among them.

6. **B** TOM OKKER—*Dutch Tennis Ace* (b. 1944)
   Thinking positive must be part of Tom Okker's arsenal.
   He burst on the tennis scene (out of his native
   Amsterdam, Holland) and became #4 in the world-wide
   rankings, as well as possibly the best Jewish player ever
   to hit an overhead. Tom won the last point against such
   players as Ashe, Nastase and Newcombe, yet his star
   shone more brightly in doubles. Teaming with a variety

of players, he either won or reached the finals in many tournaments.

7. **U** LIPMAN PIKE—*Baseball's First Pro* (1845-1893)
    "Lip" opened the floodgates. He was the first baseball player to ever be paid a salary. If he only knew what today's pros are paid. Of course, when it comes to track he wouldn't feel so bad. Today's track pros are an underpaid bunch. Pike once raced a trotting horse and won. Clarence (the horse) must have broken stride. Pike got $250. The horse? Probably an extra ration of oats.

8. **L** MARTY GLICKMAN—*Knicks Announcer* (b. 1917)
    He was the voice of the N. Y. Football Giants, N. Y. Knicks and the N. Y. Jets. But, earlier in life he let his voice be heard in a different way. Silence—heard around the world. Marty gave up his spot on the 1936 Olympic Team because of Nazi policies. Ironically, Jesse Owens took his place. The Nazi's didn't feel any better about him.

9. **E** MAURICE PODOLOFF—*NBA Prexy* (b. 1890)
    "I don't like basketball," he said. Yet Maurice became NBA prexy for 17 years. "I saved basketball," he said. It was during his presidency that the 24 second clock was introduced. He was right. The games became much more exciting when the stall was stalled. Shortly afterward, the first television contract was signed, and a few years later Podoloff retired. Asked by a reporter if he watched on TV, "Poddy" replied, "I never liked the game."

10. **I** EDWARD REULBACH—*Double Header Shutouts* (1882-1961)
    The Chicago Cubs haven't had much to shout about over the years (this year, 1985, may be the exception). But, they did have Reulbach. In 1908? Yes! 1908, Ed pitched double shutouts in a doubleheader against the Brooklyn Trolley Dodgers. He added 40 more for a total of 42 during his career.

11. **N** MARK ROTH—*Three-time Bowler of the Year* (b. 1951)
    Not everyone makes it to "Bowler of the Year." Mark Roth did it *three* times. Not every bowler wins $100,000 in a year. Mark did it in five successive years. Of course,

most good bowlers do win at least one title. Mark won 26 during an illustrious career. Only Earl Anthony had more (39), but alas, he's not Jewish!

12. **Q** HAROLD SOLOMON—*Human Backboard* (b. 1952)
They called Harold "The Human Backboard," which is a cute way of saying he's not an aggressive player. But, what about Borg the baseliner? No Borg, but a power to be reckoned with. Harold returned super smashes so well he rose to be 7th-ranked netter in the world. That was 1980. It didn't last long. He was 22nd in 1981.

13. **A** GEORGE STONE—*"Silent"* (1876-1945)
"Silent" was his nickname. His bat did the talking for him. In 1906 he won the American League batting title with a .358 average. They say he had an awkward batting style, a lefthanded hitter who got most of his hits between 2nd and 3rd. Today they'd say he went with the pitch.

14. **T** BRIAN TEACHER—*Up to 8th in Tennis* (b. 1954)
Eighth in the world was as high as he got. But that's not bad when you consider who's playing tennis these days. That was in 1981. The next year he slipped to 18th in the world. His career seemed to be dotted with occasions where he reached the finals then failed to win, thus accounting for the 8th—18th rankings.

15. **C** ELLIOTT TELTSCHER—*Up to 7th in Tennis* (b. 1959)
Tip-top tennis players have eluded the Jews. Teltscher is another who cracked the top ten but fell short of the top five. Only 25 at this writing, he still has a chance but it doesn't seem likely. He did get to #7 in 1982.

16. **J** MORRIE ARNOVICH—*So-So Ball Player* (1910-1959)
Morrie never reached anywhere near what could be characterized as stardom. He was strictly a so-so ball player. His career batting average of .287 wasn't bad.

17. **M** LARRY BROWN—*ABA, NBA Coach* (b. 1940)
Larry played his college ball at North Carolina. His pro ball was played on a variety of teams in the ABA. But it was as a coach in the ABA and NBA where Larry made a name for himself. His finest seasons were with the N. Y. Nets. But he never had a losing season with any team he coached.

18. **F** NEAL WALK—*U. of Fla. to NBA* (b. 1948)
Walk was an All-American choice while playing for
University of Florida basketball team. In 1969 the
Phoenix Suns drafted him and he played for them for
five years (1969-1974). In 1972-1973 he averaged 20.2
points per game.

19. **S** MAX ZASLOVSKY—*'48 NBA Top Scorer* (b. 1925)
The NBA only had one Jewish scoring champ, Max
Zaslovsky. He led all scorers in 1948 with a 21-point
average. He retired as the third highest all-time scorer
with 7,990 points. Today he's far down the list.

20. **G** MYRON DRABOWSKI—*"Moe"* (b. 1935)
Moe's mother was Jewish. That was good enough to get
him in this book. He came up with the Cubs in the 1950s,
forming a Dynamite Double with Dick Drott. The
dynamite never exploded. It fizzled instead and Moe
made the journey from team to team.

21. **O** NORM GREKIN—*LaSalle Standout* (b. 1930)
Norm was the MVP at the N.I.T. in 1952. He capped a
great year playing for LaSalle College of Philadelphia. I
vividly remember him playing for the Ohev Sholom
entry in the suburban Major Basketball Association. He
starred there as well, along with Eddie Lerner, Albie
Ingerman and others.

PART V

All-Time All Star Jewish Basketball Team

CENTER

Neal Walk

Born July 29, 1948, Cleveland, Ohio.

Neal attended the University of Florida and was All-American in his senior year when he ranked in the Top 10 in scoring and rebounding.

- Signed with the Phoenix Suns and played from 1969-1974.
- Moved to the New York Knicks in 1974 and played two seasons.
- He averaged over 20 points per game in 1972-73 season.
- He later played in Israel.

FORWARD

Dolph Schayes

Born May 19, 1928, New York, New York.

Definitely a candidate for greatest Jewish athlete ever.

After a very successful career at New York University, Dolph signed with the Syracuse Nationals of the National Basketball Association.

- He was Rookie of the Year in 1949.
- He was an All-Star 12 times.
- He scored almost 20,000 points, 6,979 of which were free throws.
- In 1955 Syracuse won the world championship with Schayes leading the way.
- He is a member of the Basketball Hall of Fame.

FORWARD

Arthur Heyman

Born June 24, 1942, Rockville Centre, New York.

He was a three-time All-American at Duke University and averaged over 25 points per game at Duke.

- He had a seven-year pro career. In 1964 he was named to the All-Rookie team of the National Basketball Association.
- Unfortunately, Heyman was never a great pro, although his first year he averaged over 15 points per game.

Nat Holman

Born October 18, 1896 in New York City.

He was an original Celtic and when basketball is discussed as to who is the greatest, it is impossible to leave off Nat Holman's name.

- He was with the original Celtics from 1921-1929.
- With Holman their record was absolutely mindblowing—in 1922-23, 193-11; in 1923-24, 204-11; and in 1924-25, 134-6—losing only 28 games while winning 531 in three years.
- Became one of the great coaches of the game at City College, New York.

Max Zaslowsky

Born December 7, 1925, Brooklyn, New York.

Max entered St. John's University in New York and became one of their top basketball stars.

- Entered pro ball with Chicago Stags in 1947.
- He led the league in scoring in 1948 with a 21-point average.
- He later played with the New York Knicks, Baltimore and Milwaukee.
- At the time of his retirement he was the third-highest scorer of all time in the National Basketball Association.

Arnold "Red" Auerbach

Born September 20, 1917, Brooklyn, New York.

How could anyone else be the coach of the Jewish All Star Team?

Auerbach's achievements as a coach and general manager of the Boston Celtics make him a legend in his own time.

His teams won nine National Basketball Association titles (eight in a row) during 1950-1956. *Unbelievable!*

- His coaching record is 1,037-548. Tops ever recorded.

HONORABLE MENTION

Nancy Lieberman

Born July 1, 1958, Brooklyn, New York.

At 18 years of age, she was a member of the 1976 Olympic team which won a Silver Medal in Montreal.

She attended Old Dominion University in Norfolk, Virginia, where she led that school's team to two national titles. By graduation time she was the number one women's basketball player in the world.

She went on to become a great professional star.

At this printing, she is trying to organize a new women's professional league.

PART VI

All-Time All Star Jewish Baseball Team

All-Time All Star Jewish Baseball Team

Pitchers	Sandy Koufax
	Edward Reulbach
(Relief)	Larry Sherry
Catcher	Johnny Kling (Kline)
1st Base	Henry "Hank" Greenberg
2nd Base	Charles "Buddy" Myers
3rd Base	Al Rosen
Shortstop	Andy Cohen
Left Field	Sid Gordon
Center Field	Art Shamsky
Right Field	George Stone
Owner	Barney Dreyfus

PITCHER #1

Sandy Koufax

Born December 30, 1935, in Brooklyn, New York.

The opinion of all baseball people: He is one of the greatest of all time.

- Four no-hitters.
- The youngest player ever admitted into the Baseball Hall of Fame.
- Forty shutouts.
- Oddity: he went to University of Cincinnati on a basketball scholarship.
- Spent his entire career with Los Angeles Dodgers.

PITCHER #2

Edward Reulbach

Born December 1, 1882, in Detroit, Michigan. Died July 17, 1961.

Reulbach was the only pitcher to pitch two shutouts in a doubleheader. He performed this feat during the 1908 season.

- His career record was a highly respectable 181-105.
- Once pitched four shutouts in a row.
- In 1917 he won 17, lost 4 with the Chicago Cubs.

Larry Sherry

Born July 25, 1935, in Los Angeles, California.

Born with two club feet which were operated on continually. He began walking *normally* at 12 years of age and still managed to make it to the major leagues of baseball.

- His career record, almost all in relief, was 53-44.
- Earned-run-average a respectable 3.67.
- Won the Babe Ruth Award as the outstanding player in the World Series in 1959.

CATCHER

Johnny Kling

Born November 13, 1875 in Kansas City, Missouri. Died January 31, 1947.

Considered by many to be one of the greatest catchers of all time.

- The first catcher to stand up close to the batter at all times and throw from a crouching stance.
- Played with the Chicago Cubs when they won four Pennants and two World Series in 1906, 1907, 1908, and 1910.
- Hit .271 during his 11-year career.

Henry "Hank" Greenberg

Born January 11, 1911 in New York City.

Regarded as the greatest "everyday" player of all the Jews in baseball.

- Led the American League in home runs four times.
- Led the American League in runs batted in four times.
- Career batting average of .313.
- 1,628 hits, 5,193 at bats, 1,276 RBI's.
- Challenged Ruth's record of 60 homers in 1938.
- Named the American League's Most Valuable Player in 1935.

2ND BASE

Charles "Buddy" Myers

Born in 1904 in Ellisville, Mississippi.

Never achieved great stardom but was certainly a player you would want to have on your team.

- Played in 1,923 games.
- Career batting average was .303.
- In 1935 he led the American League in hitting with a .349 average.
- In 1928 he led the American League in stolen bases with 30.
- Played for Washington and Boston during his career.

Al Rosen

Born March 1, 1925, Spartanburg, South Carolina.

Not the greatest fielder in the world, Al's rise to the majors was slow. The third try was charmed.

- Rookie of the Year in 1950. He hit 37 homers. He had 116 RBI's. His batting average was .287.
- Unanimous choice for Most Valuable Player in American League in 1953.
- Won home run championship in 1950 and 1953.
- Career batting average was .285.

SHORTSTOP

Andrew Cohen

Born October 25, 1904, Baltimore, Maryland.

Cohen actually had a rather short baseball career, playing in only 262 games.

But, being Jewish played a part in bringing him to the majors. The Giants wanted a drawing card to woo the Jewish fans.

So, we are including him on our All-Star team.

- Cohen had a .281 batting average for his career.

Sidney Gordon

Born August 13, 1918, Brooklyn, New York. Died June 16, 1975.

- 13 years in the major leagues.
- 202 career home runs.
- .283 career batting average.
- Played most of his career with the New York Giants but was traded in 1949 to the Boston Braves.

CENTER FIELD

Art Shamsky

Born October 14, 1941 in St. Louis, Missouri.

Art spent eight years in the major leagues, 1965-1972, mostly with the New York Mets.

- He once hit four home runs in four times at bat (1966) to tie a major league record.
- He hit 68 home runs during his career.
- His career batting average was .253.

George Robert Stone

Born September 3, 1876 in Lost Nation, Nebraska. Died January 6, 1945.

"Silent George" was his nickname but his bat was anything but silent.

- In 1906 he was the American League batting champ with a .358 average while with the old St. Louis Browns.
- In all, he played in the major leagues seven years.
- He had a .301 career batting average.
- He had a pretty good year in 1907 hitting .320.

OWNER

Barney Dreyfus

Born February 23, 1865, Freiberg, Germany. Died February 5, 1932.

Owned the Pittsburgh Pirates from 1900-1932.

- Some of the great players he brought to Pittsburgh were Rube Waddell, Honus Wagner and Fred Clarke.
- Pittsburgh won six National League pennants with Dreyfus as the owner.
- Pittsburgh won two World Series with Dreyfus as the owner, in 1909 and 1925.

PART VII

Jewish Population
by Countries of the World

JEWISH POPULATION OF THE WORLD

Europe

Albania	300
Austria	13,000
Belgium	41,000
Bulgaria	7,000
Czechoslovakia	12,000
Denmark	7,500
Finland	1,000
France	650,000
Germany	38,000
Gibralter	600
Great Britain	410,000
Greece	6,000
Hungary	80,000
Ireland	1,900
Italy	41,000
Luxembourg	1,000
Malta	50
Netherlands	30,000
Norway	900
Poland	6,000
Portugal	600
Romania	45,000
Spain	12,000
Sweden	17,000
Switzerland	21,000
Turkey	24,000
USSR	2,630,000
Yugoslavia	5,500

North America

Canada	305,000
Mexico	37,500
United States	5,920,890

Central America and West Indies

Barbados	70
Costa Rica	2,500
Cuba	1,500
Curacao	700
Dominican Republic	200
El Salvador	350
Guatemala	2,000
Haiti	150
Honduras	200
Jamaica	350
Nicaragua	200

Panama	2,000	Israel	3,254,000
Trinidad	300	Japan	400

South America

		Lebanon	400
		Pakistan	250
Argentina	300,000	Philippines	200
Bolivia	750	Singapore	450
Brazil	150,000	Syria	4,500
Chile	30,000	Yemen	500
Columbia	12,000		

Australia and New Zealand

Ecuador	1,000		
Paraguay	1,200	Australia	67,000
Peru	5,200	New Zealand	5,000
Surinam	500		

Africa

Uruguay	50,000		
Venezuela	15,000	Algeria	1,000
		Egypt	400

Asia

		Ethiopia	22,000
Afghanistan	200	Kenya	450
Burma	50	Libya	20
China	30	Morocco	22,000
Cyprus	30	South Africa	118,000
Hong Kong	250	Tunisia	7,000
India	8,000	Zaire	200
Indonesia	100	Zampia	400
Iran	70,000	Zimbabwe	1,960
Iraq	450	**TOTAL**	**14,527,150**

ACKNOWLEDGEMENTS AND SOURCES

The Jewish Lists
Encyclopedia Brittanica
Encyclopedia Judaica
Encyclopedia of Jews in Sports
Jewish Sports Review
Celebrity Register
Encyclopedia of Worlds Great
    Movie Stars
Photos: Movie Star News, New
    York City
and too many periodicals,
newspapers, and biographies
to mention

And finally,

Guess Who Else Is Jewish...

Guess Who's Jewish? is Len Chetkin's first attempt at writing. By far, the largest portion of his life (of 57 years) was spent slipping in and out of the fringes of show biz, singing, acting, and MCing with less than moderate success.

However, when not performing, he did manage to secure for himself a rather firm foothold in the world of business. He currently resides, with his wife Emmy, in Key West, Florida, and is at work on his next book, which, as we go to press, is a secret.